Being an Interdisciplinary Academic

"Interdisciplinarity has become pervasive in policy discourses but the arts, humanities and social sciences have yet to achieve parity in these discussions and have fewer opportunities to contribute as equal partners and—significantly—as leaders of interdisciplinary research initiatives.

Borne out of meticulous scholarship, this book seeks to address this imbalance by offering lessons that are accessible to all academics, regardless of initial training. It is a must read for anyone interested in interdisciplinary research."

—Professor Jane Ohlmeyer, *Chair of the Irish Research Council;* Director, *Trinity Long Room Hub, Arts & Humanities Research Institute;* and *Erasmus Smith's Professor of Modern History*

"As we mobilise to tackle global research challenges, this timely book reminds us that we are forging new routes through academia. This presents new challenges for the governance of our research institutions and, consequently, for the careers of those who work within them. This thoughtful account links those personal and institutional experiences and suggests practical lessons to support both individuals following an interdisciplinary path and those that shape environments for such careers."

—Professor Matthias Egger, *President of Research Council, Swiss National Science Foundation*

"Interdisciplinary research has immense potential to transform university research to meet the grand challenges facing society. But the sector is wrestling with how to create a culture that drives interdisciplinarity and enables the careers of interdisciplinary researchers to thrive.

This book draws on the experiences of researchers who have found a way to work across disciplines and provides many practical suggestions to inspire everyone from early career researchers, through to researcher developers and senior leaders."

—Dr Rachel Cowen, *Senior Lecturer and Co-Founder of the Centre for Academic and Researcher Development, University of Manchester, UK*

Catherine Lyall

Being an Interdisciplinary Academic

How Institutions Shape University Careers

Catherine Lyall
School of Social and Political Science
The University of Edinburgh
Edinburgh, UK

ISBN 978-3-030-18658-6   ISBN 978-3-030-18659-3   (eBook)
https://doi.org/10.1007/978-3-030-18659-3

This Palgrave Pivot imprint is published by the registered company Springer Nature Switzerland AG
The registered company address is: Gewerbestrasse 11, 6330 Cham, Switzerland

This "wee book" is dedicated to Gill who always has time to support others.

PREFACE

Conducting fieldwork and writing a book within a 12-month sabbatical has been, in retrospect, an ambitious task. The short-form monograph format offered by the Palgrave Pivot series has been a boon as it placed constraints on those ambitions and forced me to narrow the scope. At the same time, it has also been a frustration, as I have not had the space to explore all of the themes that arose during my study or to do full justice to the prior scholarship in this area. That said, the role of institutions in shaping interdisciplinary careers has not received great attention in the literature and I hope this shorter format will make this book more accessible to its intended audiences. I am grateful to the staff at Palgrave Macmillan for affording me this opportunity.

This book will be of interest to new academic researchers who are contemplating an interdisciplinary career and are seeking some much-needed guidance on how to avoid some of the pitfalls. In helping to support and guide these careers, more senior academic staff in their positions as Principal Investigators, mentors and supervisors, as well as those colleagues who support researcher development both within universities and other professional bodies, will find information of relevance to these roles (and I should point out that my use of the term "researcher" is not meant to imply that our attention should only be on the post-doctoral level).

The data presented here epitomise a catharsis of shared experience so, importantly, I also want to celebrate the careers and achievements of the academic colleagues who contributed to this book and allow their voices to be heard. Over the past 20 years, these individuals have pioneered a new way of working in British universities and their collective wisdom deserves to be acknowledged and communicated—but their institutions are still largely playing catch-up. To move things forward, I therefore want to stimulate discussion among university leaders and within those bodies in the public and private sector (government agencies, foundations, charities, research associations, etc.) that fund academic research and shape research policy about the impacts that their actions have on academic careers.

I want to bring the wealth of existing scholarship on interdisciplinarity to a wider readership rather than just speaking to the community of interdisciplinary scholars but it is easy to feel overwhelmed by this highly dispersed body of literature. Readability has been an important issue for me as I sought to keep this book understandable to all who seek to pursue interdisciplinary career paths or who have some other stake in them. So, I have tried to avoid too much subject-specific jargon and have essentially sidestepped much of the epistemological complexity and instead offer an "interdisciplinary primer" (see Appendix A) and substantial bibliography for those who wish to read further. Much of this literature takes a US bias where certain aspects, such as the tenure process and postgraduate training models, are less applicable to universities in other countries. The empirical emphasis of this current work offers a counterbalance to this US dominance but nevertheless deals with generally applicable themes and concerns.

My style as an academic researcher, and therefore the tenor of this book, is to concentrate more on suggestions for improvements, based on practical experiences derived from empirical data, rather than on explanatory theories or descriptive taxonomies—and, in doing so, to ensure that the data are presented in a way that reaches a breadth of potential audiences.

Despite the focus on this mode of working in recent years, interdisciplinarity continues to present seemingly intractable problems for our universities and for the people who work in them and with them. Collectively, we could create better opportunities for institutional leaders and research funders who promote interdisciplinarity to hear from those who actually practise interdisciplinary research about their experiences and desires as academic researchers. In listening to both groups during the course of my study, I have been trying to model the type of behaviour that I am encouraging among these institutions. I certainly do not claim to have the answers to all of these problems but this book might just provoke smart people to think about a few more solutions.

Edinburgh, UK   Catherine Lyall

ACKNOWLEDGEMENTS

I could not have completed this task without the help of many people. Alice Hague's patient tracing of my potential sample of awardholders gave my research firm foundations. Next, I am very grateful to Moyra Guilar and Eileen Mothersole for their fast and accurate transcribing of interviews, although I imagine neither of them wants to hear the word "interdisciplinary" ever again. Academic writing (and reading) demands good indexing and I could not be more fortunate than to have Moyra Forrest as my indexer.

My fieldwork was enabled through several funding sources including EU COST Action Intrepid (TD1408) Short Term Scientific Mission and the University of Edinburgh's College of Arts, Humanities and Social Science Susan Manning Award for Outstanding Mentorship and School of Social and Political Science Strategic Research Support Fund. I am most appreciative of this assistance and the travel to interviews that I was able to undertake as a result.

These interviews would not have happened without the generous participation of busy academic colleagues who were willing to give their time to contribute to my data collection. I would also like to acknowledge the help of the Vice Rectors' personal assistants who managed to find me space in their diaries. I especially thank Katrien Maes, Deputy Secretary General, League of European Research Universities (LERU) for generously hosting my visit to the LERU offices and for her insights into their study on interdisciplinarity and the twenty-first-century research-intensive university.

I am indebted to Laura Meagher (Technology Development Group) both for her enthusiastic support during the writing process and for our much longer-term collaboration; significantly, some of our earliest work together generated the initial study that underpins this book. Katrine Lindvig (University of Copenhagen) generously allowed me to use her concept of the "loud and soft voices" of interdisciplinarity. Justyna Bandola-Gill, Gill Haddow, Katrine Lindvig, Laura Meagher and Steve Yearley were my first readers who all pushed me to do better and I could not have reached this stage without them. Beyond my immediate colleagues, I would like to thank Gabriele Bammer, Machiel Keestra, Julie Klein, Christian Pohl and Rick Szostak for inviting me in to their networks, sharing their knowledge and showing me that scholarship on interdisciplinarity does indeed have its own "invisible college". I am grateful, too, to the three anonymous reviewers of my original proposal for their encouragement and suggestions.

Finally, I have some more personal "thank yous": to my friend John for use of his quiet study when I needed to get to grips with my data analysis; to Corinna at Wellspring for helping me to keep this project in perspective; and to my partner Richard for taking care of general life logistics, including numerous early morning and late night trips to the railway station and airport.

CONTENTS

ABBREVIATIONS

ECR	Early Career Researcher (or early stage researcher)
ESRC	Economic and Social Research Council
GCRF	Global Challenges Research Fund
GRC	Global Research Council
IDR	Interdisciplinary Research
LERU	League of European Research Universities
LWEC	Living with Environmental Change
MRC	Medical Research Council
NERC	Natural Environment Research Council
NGO	Non-Governmental Organisation
NHS	National Health Service
OECD	Organisation for Economic Co-operation and Development
PI	Principal Investigator
RAE	Research Assessment Exercise
RCUK	Research Councils UK
REF	Research Excellence Framework
STS	Science and Technology Studies
UKRI	UK Research and Innovation

ABOUT THE AUTHOR

Catherine Lyall is Professor of Science and Public Policy at the University of Edinburgh where, despite a first degree in chemistry, she holds a position in the School of Social and Political Science. Her career at Edinburgh has progressed from part-time Research Officer to Personal Chair via numerous research contracts within grant-funded research centres and a period as Associate Dean for Research Careers.

LIST OF TABLES

CHAPTER 1

Introduction: Mixed Messages for the Interdisciplinary Research Community

Interdisciplinary research may have become a cornerstone of research policy internationally (e.g. European Commission 2007; National Science Foundation 2006; National Academy of Sciences 2005; Bammer 2013) but is still widely regarded as not having achieved its full potential (League of European Research Universities, LERU 2016). This limited achievement is due in large part to persistent—and well-documented obstacles—within academic structures traditionally built upon single disciplines (e.g. LERU 2016; Lyall et al. 2011, 2013; Lyall and Fletcher 2013). The core purpose of this book is to investigate what this rift between rhetoric and reality implies for those who wish to either foster, or to pursue, interdisciplinary academic careers.

In what follows, I present empirical data collected through a series of interviews with individuals who practise interdisciplinary research in contradistinction to those who promote it. What this reveals is a manifest misalignment between the high-level strategic pronouncements that institutions, such as universities and research funders, make about wanting to support interdisciplinarity and the actuality of what it means to be an interdisciplinary researcher trying to forge an academic career and scholarly identity. While the vision and strategy might exist, operationalising those in practice was regarded by fellow academics as being far less developed, highlighting the mismatch between interdisciplinary expectations and the prevailing norms of discipline-based scholarship.

© The Author(s) 2019
C. Lyall, *Being an Interdisciplinary Academic*,
https://doi.org/10.1007/978-3-030-18659-3_1

One might be forgiven for assuming that "interdisciplinarity" is the new zeitgeist in academia given the apparent attention paid to it by funders and policymakers (e.g. Global Research Council 2016). Nevertheless, implementation of interdisciplinary research is by no means universal.[1] While there are undoubtedly pockets of excellence (or at least good practice), one could reasonably argue that the university sector in the UK is still approaching interdisciplinarity as "a trend rather than a real transition" (Rhoten 2004).

The downsides of interdisciplinary research within an academic context are well established (e.g. Lowe et al. 2013) and it has certainly not achieved the status of a mainstream activity within British universities. Academic recognition, in the form of promotion, prizes or membership of professional bodies, still predominantly comes from established disciplines. The majority of the world's leading research-intensive universities are still organised along disciplinary lines. Disciplines help to organise knowledge for teaching and for quality assessment purposes. The more one strays outside disciplinary frames, the harder it may be to demonstrate one's depth and pertinence of expertise and hence to pursue what is conventionally deemed a "successful" academic career.

Interdisciplinary research and innovation have become conclusively linked in the minds of policymakers and research funders (e.g. UKRI 2018). There is, today, a general consensus within national and international research policy that many striking research advances take place at the boundaries between disciplines, leading in some cases to the emergence of new fields (e.g. nanotechnology, synthetic biology). At the same time, issues of global concern, such as climate change or ageing populations, demand that we find new approaches to combine insights from different disciplines and bodies of knowledge. So, in a sense, this provides an answer to the question: *why* do interdisciplinary research. However, for every policy statement and publication promoting this "new"[2] mode of research, there are detractors (e.g. Abbott 2001; Jacobs and Frickel 2009) who still value a narrower perspective, arguing that this brings greater depth of insight. This theme of breadth versus depth is fundamental and one to which I return at various points in the book.

---

[1] Interdisciplinary teaching is also much less prevalent in the UK and Europe than it is in the US although this situation is gradually beginning to change (Lyall et al. 2015).

[2] This is, of course, not a new term with the first use of "interdisciplinarity" often being traced back to the Social Sciences Research Council in the 1920s and then expanded upon by OECD (Apostel 1972).

Even more significant for the theme of this book is the question of *who* conducts this research. Modern universities still predominantly privilege disciplinary over interdisciplinary work (Aldrich 2014, p. 61). Academics who come from a strong disciplinary foundation, work in a team-based interdisciplinary collaboration but can then return to their discipline, face fewer career obstacles than those who do not associate strongly with a single discipline and who have been trained from the outset to work across disciplines (see e.g. Hess 2018). Arguably, the former group sits much more comfortably within existing institutional governance structures.[3] The latter group, those who do not have an immediately obvious disciplinary "home", experience rather different impediments to their academic careers and are the primary focus of this book.

Our identities, and our career progression, as academics seem irrefutably bound to disciplines (in the context of both our research and teaching). This leads to the "paradox of interdisciplinarity" (Weingart 2000; Woelert and Millar 2013) where interdisciplinary research is often encouraged at policy level but poorly rewarded by funding instruments and academic structures.[4] In promulgating greater interdisciplinary capacity building, do we then risk training future generations of scholars who will feel like strangers in their home departments, inhabiting uncomfortable liminal spaces within their institutions?

The British Academy (2016, p. 10) has urged its constituency to "develop an academic home and remain attached to it" even while being encouraged to connect with those working in different disciplines. In contrast, other commentators embrace much earlier engagement with interdisciplinarity, arguing that

> [p]ostponing interdisciplinary work to the time a researcher is well established means that such research is generally pursued as a side activity....this means that the inventiveness and creativity of younger scholars is discouraged from going into interdisciplinary work, slowing down this work, making it intellectually and practically less attractive. (Sperber 2003, quoted in Henry 2005)

---

[3] I define key governance institutions in this context as the universities as employers, funding bodies as drivers of interdisciplinary research, and professional groups such as the British Academy as guardians of tradition and upholders of quality. See also Chap. 3, Footnote 1.

[4] Evidenced, for example, by research using data from the Australian Research Council that demonstrated that the greater the degree of interdisciplinarity, the lower the probability of grant proposals receiving funding (Bromham et al. 2016).

There is an expanding literature on the hazards of interdisciplinarity for early career researchers trying to foster an academic career (e.g. Golde and Gallagher 1999; Graybill et al. 2006; Pfirman and Begg 2012; Martin and Pfirman 2017). Interdisciplinary research has been deemed "career suicide" for young researchers (Bothwell 2016) but systematic investigation of interdisciplinarity's longer-term effects on academic careers is sparse (Leahey et al. 2017; Millar 2013). One of the central motivations for writing this book is that the UK research community apparently finds it difficult to recruit adequately experienced interdisciplinary researchers (LWEC 2012). In contrast, Callard and Fitzgerald (2015, p. 12) have suggested that "the risks of interdisciplinarity aren't what they used to be" and that these negative opinions are "overemphasized". Consequently, one of my key goals has been to explore whether well-established truisms about interdisciplinary careers do indeed still hold true in an area of research policy where researchers—and especially those at the start of their academic career—receive very mixed messages.

Avoiding Terminological Minefields

"Interdisciplinarity" is a word that denotes a spectrum of experience: while the term may have become ubiquitous, it is also contested, so that it is indeed "a term that everyone invokes and none understands" (Callard and Fitzgerald 2015, p. 4), a "catch-all" term (Bammer 2016), often used imprecisely in a variety of contexts.

Research policy (and indeed the policy community at large) invariably makes the mistake of talking about "interdisciplinarity" as if it is one, unified approach to research. While attempts are being made to bring greater coherence and integration to the field (Bammer 2013), in reality it is much more nuanced. Experiences of interdisciplinary research may be very different depending on whether it takes place between proximate disciplines (i.e. within the social sciences, the natural sciences, the medical sciences, or the arts and humanities) or involves much more distant disciplines, for example, spanning the social sciences and natural sciences. This prompts Barry and Born (2013, p. 5) to ask how we might better understand interdisciplinarity as "a field of differences".

Taken to extremes, contestation around terminology in this field can verge on "theological hair-splitting" (Rylance 2015) so, rather than revisit these debates in great detail, I propose to adopt the following broad definition:

> Interdisciplinary research (IDR) is a mode of research by teams or individuals that integrates information, data, techniques, tools, perspectives, concepts, and/or theories from two or more disciplines or bodies of specialized knowledge to advance fundamental understanding or to solve problems whose solutions are beyond the scope of a single discipline or area of research practice. (National Academy of Sciences 2005, p. 188)

For the purposes of what follows, I simply regard interdisciplinary research as occurring where the contributions of the various disciplines are integrated to provide holistic or systemic outcomes.[5] For simplicity, I use the shorthand term "interdisciplinary" throughout but recognise that many of the themes of this book apply equally well to "transdisciplinary" research and to "team science". For readers who are less familiar with the literature in this field, I have included an "interdisciplinary primer" on these and related topics in the form of a short annotated reading list in Appendix A.[6]

Interdisciplinary research is not just about practical, applied, action research, it is also one way in which disciplines evolve. Challenging intellectual debates take place at the boundaries of existing disciplines and in the gaps between them. Distinctions can be drawn between long-term, interdisciplinary involvement for "academic" reasons (e.g. to enable a discipline to move into new areas of research) and the shorter-term, situational interest where the primary aim is problem oriented and discipline-related outputs are less central to project design. We have discussed this in more detail elsewhere (Bruce et al. 2004; Lyall et al. 2011, pp. 14–18) and have termed these different (but not necessarily mutually exclusive) approaches:

> "*Academically oriented interdisciplinarity*" to define research that aims to further the expertise and competence of academic disciplines themselves, e.g. through developments in methodology which enable new issues to be addressed or new disciplines or sub-disciplines to be formed.
>
> "*Problem focused interdisciplinarity*" to define research that addresses issues of social, technical and/or policy relevance with less emphasis on discipline related academic outcomes.

---

[5] Readers who want to take this back to first principles and ask "what is a discipline" may find Krishnan (2009) a useful entry point.

[6] For Spanish readers, I also highly recommend the anthology edited by Vienni et al. (2015) prepared for the same purpose and described (in English and Spanish) in their blog https://i2insights.org/2016/10/25/interdisciplinarity-readings/ (accessed 7/1/19).

These two modes of interdisciplinary research are appropriate to different types of research question and will require differing combinations of expertise in researchers. Significantly, both types of research suggest that the academic world needs to learn to ascribe greater importance to the integration and application of knowledge (Frodeman 2014) and not simply to cherish the traditional scholarship of new discoveries within a single discipline (Lattuca 2001).

OBJECTIVES OF THE BOOK

This book presents new empirical data drawn from a series of career history interviews with a sample of interdisciplinary researchers trained in the UK over the past two decades. The research on which this book is based initially set out to answer the question "How are interdisciplinary academic careers developed and supported?" although undoubtedly ended up answering the more normative question "How *should* institutions develop and support interdisciplinary academic careers?"

My principal aim is to inform the behaviours of individuals and the practices of institutions engaged in promoting interdisciplinary research. My goal is not to build a grand theory of interdisciplinarity. Nor is it to test the theories of others. Instead, I want to be able to speak authoritatively about the status of interdisciplinary academic researchers, and the career challenges they face, in order to improve upon current practice.

In doing so, I identify some of the steps that the research community[7] could take if we are to build a cadre of resilient interdisciplinary researchers. These individuals need to be able to craft their research trajectories in ways that allow them to develop academic reputations based on a coherent profile of skills so that they are better equipped to tackle the complex, multidimensional research problems posed by today's world and whatever futures we might face. Changing the academic landscape will have significant consequences (Lyall 2013). Doing so will require us to reflect on the nature of the modern university, and related institutions of governance, in ways that question current institutional logics.

The niche that this book occupies in the literature is a small but growing one on the governance of interdisciplinarity (e.g. Weingart 2014;

---

[7] Broadly defined to include stakeholders from research funders and policy bodies as well as those employed by universities. Of course, not all of these stakeholders will themselves be interdisciplinary researchers.

Woelert 2015; Donina et al. 2017). The scholarly literature abounds with case studies of interdisciplinary research experiences so one might reasonably ask whether we have indeed reached "peak interdisciplinarity" (Frodeman 2017, p. 5) and how we can justify yet another book on the topic.[8] My fieldwork prior to writing suggests that considerable confusion about the merits and demerits of an interdisciplinary academic career still prevails. Moreover, our existing body of knowledge is disjointed and dispersed across a wide array of journals and other publications, which renders it less accessible to newcomers and means that, as a research community, we do not have an easily comprehensible "canon" that would enable us to accumulate shared learning about interdisciplinary careers efficiently.

Facilitating interdisciplinarity in universities has long been considered an institutional problem but we lack detailed examination of researchers' experiences of the "organisational conditions" of interdisciplinary research (Sá 2008). The situation is exacerbated by the lack of leadership to bring about organisational change (ibid.) There can also be a tendency not to absorb prior knowledge on interdisciplinarity[9] and a lack of recognition of existing scholarship (see e.g. Szostak 2015). I want to shift the focus onto the institutional level, rather than on the wealth of more individualised case studies of discrete programmes or projects that already exists. As noted in the Preface, the intentionally short format offered by the Palgrave Pivot series affords a valuable opportunity to write something in a style that should be more accessible, recognising that it is often a challenge for mixed audiences to read the academic interdisciplinary literature in great depth (Klein 2010, p. 9). This is not, therefore, a book about how to "do" interdisciplinary research per se but is, most definitely, about how to "govern" interdisciplinarity and better support interdisciplinary careers.

This is, of course, a potentially immense topic. In order to narrow the focus, I concentrate primarily on UK universities (using a smaller selection of interviews with northern European universities to explore what contrasts and comparisons they might bring to the data[10]). I have taken the premise of "starting where you are" (Lofland and Lofland 1995) to

[8] See www.transdisciplinarity.ch/en/td-net/Publikationen/Publikationsradar.html (accessed 7/1/19) for a yearly analysis of publication activities in the field of inter- and transdisciplinarity.

[9] See, for example, *Nature* supplement on interdisciplinarity (*Nature* 525, 305; 2015) and subsequent letters to *Nature*.

[10] While acknowledging differences between university governance in Anglo-Saxon and European countries (van der Zwaan 2017, p. 41).

enlarge upon previous work on researcher development and the management of interdisciplinary research in order to scrutinise the pervasive belief that interdisciplinary careers are difficult to build and sustain within British universities (e.g. Lyall et al. 2011, 2013; Lyall and Meagher 2012; Lyall and Fletcher 2013).

Listening to the Loud and Soft Voices of Interdisciplinarity

Albert et al. (2017, p. 88) use the concept of "decoupling" (borrowed from neo-institutional theories, e.g. Bromley and Powell 2012) to explain discrepancies between institutional policies and the actual practice of interdisciplinarity within organisations. Lindvig (2017, pp. 147–149) looks at this decoupling or misalignment in a different way by contrasting the "loud and performative voice" of interdisciplinarity that is present at strategic, institutional levels with the "quiet and productive voice" of those engaged in its daily practice.

In the chapters that follow, I discuss individual and institutional practices concerning interdisciplinary careers, listening to both the loud and the soft voices[11] to explain some of the paradoxes that exist within the current institutional governance of interdisciplinarity.[12] It is not possible to discuss the reasons for pursuing an academic career in interdisciplinarity in isolation from the institutional issues and policies that shape or constrain such career options and choices. What becomes clear is that the personal and the institutional are intertwined. Furthermore, by taking this twinned approach, it is evident in the contrasts arising from these first-person accounts that institutions are not listening to the soft voices: interviewees complain that nobody within their university's leadership acknowledges their expertise as interdisciplinarians or recognises "some of the really quite mundane barriers" (Julia). There is, as discussed later, a perceived generational issue where universities are seen as only listening to the "loud" voices of their professors who are often "the least interdisciplinary people" (Gina). All the research-intensive universities who participated in this study espoused very similar strategic research themes or

[11] See Appendix B for a discussion of how I have used direct, anonymised quotations from my interviewees in this text.

[12] Paradoxes, according to Granovetter (1973), are "a welcome antidote to theories which explain everything all too neatly".

"grand challenges" (Kuhlmann and Rip 2018) around artificial intelligence (AI), data science, climate change, ageing and so on, exhibiting what Crow and Dabars (2015, p. 118) have termed "institutional isomorphism". Yet, with respect to institutional behaviours, as awardholders attested "the 'same old' isn't actually fixing the world's problems" (Gina).

Methods and Sampling Frame

During the period 1999–2008, the UK Research Councils funded over 200 interdisciplinary PhD studentships across the social/environmental sciences and the social/medical sciences[13] through two dedicated funding schemes designed to build interdisciplinary research capacity. Many of these PhD graduates are now well established in their academic careers. Core data for this study were gathered via semi-structured biographical interviews with a sample of these awardholders. These "awardholder interviews" sought to explore career milestones and other significant events, including perceived career enablers and barriers, in an attempt to understand how interdisciplinary academic research careers develop and progress. A further set of "leadership interviews" with Vice Rectors of Research in a sample drawn from research-intensive universities then sought to probe how such universities' vision for interdisciplinarity might impact on career development. What follows in the subsequent chapters is an essentially narrative-led account arising from these data.[14]

The research draws on our previous evaluation reports of the ESRC/NERC and ESRC/MRC studentship schemes (Meagher and Lyall 2005, 2009) but is not a longitudinal study, as I have not intentionally involved the same respondents whom we included in the original evaluations. Nor is it a formal follow-up to, or evaluation of, the LERU report (LERU 2016) on interdisciplinarity from which the leadership sample was drawn as explained in Appendix B.

Critics might ask about the awardholders who did not complete their PhD, or who wanted to pursue a career outside of academia or—most

[13] Funded by the Economic and Social Research Council (ESRC) and the Natural Environment Research Council (NERC) and by the Economic and Social Research Council and the Medical Research Council (MRC) respectively.

[14] The empirical data presented in this book derive from 32 qualitative interviews. A detailed account of the research design, an explanation of the anonymisation process and a summary of the demographic profiles of the 22 awardholder interviewees are included in Appendix B.

significantly—those who wanted an academic post but could not secure one or who perhaps completed a post-doctoral position but did not secure a subsequent post and left academia disillusioned. There is also a much larger pool of potential interviewees who have pursued interdisciplinary careers within UK universities but who were not funded via one of these joint Research Council interdisciplinary studentships. My response to these arguments is that the sampling process yielded a targeted group of informants who were particularly sensitised to the topic from the earliest stages of their academic careers and who had managed to continue in academic employment and were therefore well positioned to make observations about the development of such careers. The lessons that these interviews offer should be equally applicable to those from the wider interdisciplinary research community as they are not subject specific.

In asking respondents to reflect on past experiences I also have to acknowledge not just the role of memory but also how we reconstruct and account for events that happened in our past. One might expect selectivity to have been a particular issue with senior research leaders who were speaking on behalf of their institutions although in several cases the conversations felt quite personal; as discussed later they often spoke from their own relatively narrow disciplinary experiences. Awardholder interviewees appreciated the security of anonymity in order to speak candidly and some talked quite passionately about personal issues that were very much to the fore at the time of the interview. Finally, I should record that the University and College Union industrial action that took place in the UK in the early part of 2018 did influence, in some instances, when and where interviews took place and may also have affected how some interviewees responded about matters relating to their university employment at that time.

PLAN OF THE BOOK

I am reminded of the quote with which I opened my PhD thesis (Lyall 2005):

> Shall the practitioner stay on the high, hard ground where he can practice rigorously … but where he is constrained to deal with problems of relatively little social importance? Or shall he descend into the swamp where he can engage the most important or challenging problems if he is willing to forsake technical rigor? (Schön 1983, p. 42)

The "hard ground", in this case, might represent a series of relatively safe institutional strategies and quick interdisciplinary fixes promoted by the loud voices. In contrast, the soft voices are trying to navigate the "swamp" in order to carve out meaningful interdisciplinary careers.

So I begin, in Chap. 2, by presenting some of the rich data from my awardholder interviews to help us understand how interdisciplinary academic careers are established. Chapter 3 shifts the focus on to the roles that institutions play in this process of shaping interdisciplinary careers.

One of the key misalignments that became evident when I started my leadership interviews was the question of the optimal point for academic careers to make this turn towards interdisciplinarity. Chapter 4 introduces some concepts around training as socialisation and not simply skills acquisition, drawing briefly on the sociology of scientific knowledge literature to discuss implications for academic capacity building.

In Chap. 5 I discuss another misalignment between institutions' top down approaches to interdisciplinarity versus the bottom up, grassroots interdisciplinarity favoured by many of my awardholder interviewees. This introduces the idea of "slow research" (Slow Science Academy 2010) and the question of how institutions might facilitate some of the unanticipated encounters that so often appear to characterise interdisciplinary careers.

As I have already noted, there is a substantial body of literature and tacit expertise about interdisciplinarity and its potential shortcomings that is not yet adequately institutionalised. We could essentially remedy many of the problems associated with interdisciplinary research (such as peer review) if we were truly committed to doing this. In order to do so we need to move from the current focus on individual cases—those admirable, intricate, theory-driven analyses—and look instead at the bigger story. We need to go beyond the much-vaunted barriers to interdisciplinarity and instead take a more systemic look at interdisciplinary practices and the driving forces behind them. Chapter 6 therefore proposes two new logics that could turn interdisciplinary research from something that is, to a great extent, largely symbolic into a more systemic approach. This penultimate chapter recommends some practical steps that institutions could take in order to affirm their commitment to interdisciplinary careers.

Throughout, at the end of each chapter, I offer a set of "Talking Points" to summarise the key messages and encourage readers (academics, their university leaders, funders and other stakeholders) to consider the implications of these "misalignments" in order to enhance the practical value of these findings to their own individual and institutional settings. Chapter 7 concludes the book with a series of practical recommendations for academic researchers, their funders and their university leaders that will enable both interdisciplinary careers and those focused on traditional disciplines to be more equally valued within the modern academy.

My Role as Researcher

I am interested in this topic of interdisciplinary careers both as an object of academic study and as a reflection of my personal experience of academic life. As a chemistry graduate with postgraduate degrees in science and technology policy (Master's degree) and science and technology studies (STS) (PhD), I have never felt a strong disciplinary affiliation. Nor, given the nuanced difference between "policy" and "studies" in the titles of my postgraduate degrees, have I ever felt a particularly good "fit" with the more sociologically informed STS environment in which I have worked for the past 20 years. Factor in a rather less conventional academic career that saw me employed by a university for the first time as I approached the middle part of my career, at which point I completed a part-time PhD, followed by a very long period on temporary contracts prior to finally joining the "permanent" staff on promotion to personal chair (full professor). I have only ever worked for one university, which has also inevitably coloured my experiences, and for much of this time worked in a research centre that branded itself as "interdisciplinary" but did little to reflect on what that meant or how that might impact on the developing careers of its staff. For these reasons, my own personal experience is inevitably interwoven with the findings. Perhaps I am now at a stage in my career where I feel less need to apologise for this.

I had approached these interviews as essentially "interviewing one's peers" (Platt 1981) but it was Julia who pointed out that interviewees saw me as a senior woman and that it would have been different had I been a more junior researcher: "There is also the issue that because you're a professor and you're a woman then people naturally turn to you for advice." I was quite conscious of not turning these interviews into mentoring sessions but several of them, most notably with the women, seemed to end on that note. Was it significant that two of the women who were on maternity leave when we spoke said that the interview "had been like therapy" and how it had been helpful to think about these career issues before they returned to work?

Julia, herself, said at the end: "This is more of an advice interview, it's very helpful to me." Julia was not alone in observing that no one had ever asked for her views on this topic before and it was evident that interdisciplinary researchers were not always receiving the quality of support and mentoring that they needed from their own institutions.

This book is obviously set within a much wider context of change globally within the university sector (see e.g. van der Zwaan 2017). Interdisciplinarity is also an area that can generate quite strong emotions (both pro and anti), possibly linked to the issue of academic identity (and potential loss thereof) as discussed in the next chapter. I adopt a pragmatic viewpoint that, *if* we are going to conduct interdisciplinary research (and I do believe that there are both intellectual *and* societal reasons for doing so), then we should acknowledge the administrative and personal costs of doing so within our current institutions and do what we can to lower these barriers.

In the interests of accessibility, this book is not aimed at readers from any particular discipline although the nature of the dataset and my own personal background do result in a greater focus on interdisciplinarity that spans the social, medical and natural sciences rather than on the arts and humanities but this is avowedly not intended to exclude those disciplines from the discussion. I want this book to be widely read and generally applicable so have to accept that this may open it up to criticism for being too "general". That sense of ambiguity is, after all, an everyday feature of interdisciplinary life.

References

Abbott, A. 2001. *Chaos of Disciplines*. Chicago: University of Chicago Press.

Albert, M., E. Paradis, and A. Kuper. 2017. Interdisciplinary Fantasy. Social Scientists and Humanities Scholars Working in Faculties of Medicine. In *Investigating Interdisciplinary Research: Theory and Practice Across Disciplines*, ed. B. Prainsack, S. Frickel, and M. Albert. New Brunswick, NJ: Rutgers University Press.

Aldrich, John. 2014. *Interdisciplinarity*. Oxford: Oxford University Press.

Apostel, Leo. 1972. *Interdisciplinarity Problems of Teaching and Research in Universities*. Paris: OECD.

Bammer, Gabriele. 2013. *Disciplining Interdisciplinarity. Integration and Implementation Sciences for Researching Complex Real-World Problems*. Canberra: ANU E Press.

———. 2016. Moving Interdisciplinary Research Forward: Top Down Organising Force Needed to Help Classify Diverse Practices. *LSE Impact Blog*, February 11. http://blogs.lse.ac.uk/impactofsocialsciences/2016/02/11/moving-interdisciplinary-research-forward/. Accessed 24 January 2019.

Barry, Andrew, and Georgina Born. 2013. Interdisciplinarity. Reconfigurations of the Social and Natural Sciences. In *Interdisciplinarity. Reconfigurations of the Social and Natural Sciences*, ed. Andrew Barry and Georgina Born, 1–56. Abingdon: Routledge.

Bothwell, E. 2016. Multidisciplinary Research 'Career Suicide' for Junior Academics. *Times Higher Education*, May 3.

British Academy. 2016. *Crossing Paths: Interdisciplinary Institutions, Careers, Education and Applications*. London: British Academy.

Bromham, L., R. Dinnage, and X. Hua. 2016. Interdisciplinary Research Has Consistently Lower Funding Success. *Nature* 534 (7609): 684–687.

Bromley, Patricia, and Walter W. Powell. 2012. From Smoke and Mirrors to Walking the Talk: Decoupling in the Contemporary World. *The Academy of Management Annals* 6 (1): 483–530.

Bruce, A., C. Lyall, J. Tait, and R. Williams. 2004. Interdisciplinary Integration in the Fifth Framework Programme. *Futures* 36 (4): 457–470.

Callard, F., and D. Fitzgerald. 2015. *Rethinking Interdisciplinarity Across the Social Sciences and Neurosciences*. Basingstoke, UK: Palgrave.

Crow, M., and W. Dabars. 2015. *Designing the New American University*. Baltimore: Johns Hopkins University Press.

Donina, Davide, Marco Seeber, and Stefano Paleari. 2017. Inconsistencies in the Governance of Interdisciplinarity: The Case of the Italian Higher Education System. *Science and Public Policy* 44 (6): 865–875.

European Commission. 2007. *FP7 Taking European Research to the Forefront*. Brussels: European Commission.

Frodeman, Robert. 2014. *Sustainable Knowledge*. Basingstoke, UK: Palgrave.

———. 2017. The Future of Interdisciplinarity. In *The Oxford Handbook of Interdisciplinarity*, ed. Robert Frodeman, Julie Thompson Klein, and Roberto C.S. Pacheco, 3–8. Oxford: Oxford University Press.

Global Research Council. 2016. Statement of Principles on Interdisciplinarity. https://www.globalresearchcouncil.org/fileadmin/documents/GRC_Publications/Statement_of_Principles_on_Interdisciplinarity.pdf. Accessed 24 January 2019.

Golde, Chris M., and Hanna Alix Gallagher. 1999. The Challenges of Conducting Interdisciplinary Research in Traditional Doctoral Programs. *Ecosystems* 2: 281–285.

Granovetter, Mark S. 1973. The Strength of Weak Ties. *American Journal of Sociology* 78 (6): 1360–1380.

Graybill, J.K., S. Dooling, V. Shandas, J. Withey, A. Greve, and G.L. Simon. 2006. A Rough Guide to Interdisciplinarity: Graduate Student Perspectives. *BioScience* 56 (9): 757–763.

Henry, Stuart. 2005. Disciplinary Hegemony Meets Interdisciplinary Ascendancy: Can Interdisciplinary/Integrative Studies Survive, and If So, How? *Issues in Integrative Studies* 23: 1–37.

Hess, Andi. 2018. Two Types of Interdisciplinary Scholarship. *Integration and Implementation Insights*, February 6. https://i2insights.org/2018/02/06/two-types-of-interdisciplinarity/#andi-hess. Accessed 24 January 2019.

Jacobs, Jerry A., and Scott Frickel. 2009. Interdisciplinarity: A Critical Assessment. *Annual Review of Sociology* 35: 43–65. https://doi.org/10.1146/annurev-soc-070308-115954.

Klein, Julie Thompson. 2010. *Creating Interdisciplinary Campus Cultures*. San Francisco: Jossey Bass.

Krishnan, Armin. 2009. What Are Academic Disciplines? Some Observations on the Disciplinarity vs. Interdisciplinarity Debate. ESRC National Centre for Research Methods NCRM Working Paper Series 03/09.

Kuhlmann, Stefan, and Arie Rip. 2018. Next-Generation Innovation Policy and Grand Challenges. *Science and Public Policy* 45 (4): 448–454.

Lattuca, Lisa R. 2001. *Creating Interdisciplinarity*. Nashville: Vanderbilt University Press.

League of European Research Universities. 2016. *Interdisciplinarity and the 21st Century Research-Intensive University*. Leuven: LERU.

Leahey, E., C.M. Beckman, and T.L. Stanko. 2017. Prominent but Less Productive: The Impact of Interdisciplinarity on Scientists' Research. *Administrative Science Quarterly* 62 (1): 105–139.

Lindvig, Katrine. 2017. Creating Interdisciplinarity Within Monodisciplinary Structures. PhD Thesis, University of Copenhagen.

Lofland, J., and L.H. Lofland. 1995. *Starting Where You Are*. Belmont, CA: Wadsworth.

Lowe, Philip, Jeremy Phillipson, and Katy Wilkinson. 2013. Why Social Scientists Should Engage with Natural Scientists. *Contemporary Social Science: Journal of the Academy of Social Sciences* 8 (3): 207–222.

LWEC. 2012. Living with Environmental Change Short form Skills Framework. https://nerc.ukri.org/skills/postgrad/policy/skillsreview/2012/skills-framework/. Accessed 7 January 2019.

Lyall, C. 2005. Concurrent Power. The Role of Policy Networks in the Multi-level Governance of Science and Innovation in Scotland. PhD, University of Edinburgh.

———. 2013. The Institutional Challenges of Changing the Academic Landscape. In *Disciplining Interdisciplinarity. Integration and Implementation Sciences for Researching Complex Real-World Problems*, ed. G. Bammer. Canberra: ANU E Press.

Lyall, Catherine, and I. Fletcher. 2013. Experiments in Interdisciplinary Capacity-Building: The Successes and Challenges of Large-Scale Interdisciplinary Investments. *Science and Public Policy* 40: 1–7.

Lyall, C., and L. Meagher. 2012. A Masterclass in Interdisciplinarity: Research into Practice in Training the Next Generation of Interdisciplinary Researchers. *Futures* 44 (6): 608–617.

Lyall, C., A. Bruce, J. Tait, and L. Meagher. 2011. *Interdisciplinary Research Journeys. Practical Strategies for Capturing Creativity.* London: Bloomsbury Academic.

Lyall, Catherine, Ann Bruce, Wendy Marsden, and Laura Meagher. 2013. The Role of Funding Agencies in Creating Interdisciplinary Knowledge. *Science and Public Policy* 40: 62–71.

Lyall, C., L. Meagher, J. Bandola, and A. Kettle. 2015. Interdisciplinary Provision in Higher Education: Current and Future Challenges. Report to Higher Education Academy.

Martin, Paula J.S., and Stephanie Pfirman. 2017. Facilitating Interdisciplinary Scholars. In *The Oxford Handbook of Interdisciplinarity*, ed. Robert Frodeman, Julie Thompson Klein, and C.S. Robert Pacheco, 586–600. Oxford: Oxford University Press.

Meagher, Laura, and Catherine Lyall. 2005. Evaluation of the ESRC/NERC Interdisciplinary Research Studentship Scheme. Report to ESRC.

———. 2009. Evaluation of ESRC/MRC Interdisciplinary Research Studentship and Post-Doctoral Fellowship Scheme. Report to ESRC.

Millar, M.M. 2013. Interdisciplinary Research and the Early Career: The Effect of Interdisciplinary Dissertation Research on Career Placement and Publication Productivity of Doctoral Graduates in the Sciences. *Research Policy* 42 (5): 1152–1164.

National Academy of Sciences. 2005. *Facilitating Interdisciplinary Research.* Washington, DC: National Academies Press.

National Science Foundation. 2006. *Investing in America's Future Strategic Plan FY 2006–2011.* Washington, DC: National Science Foundation.

Pfirman, Stephanie, and Melissa Begg. 2012. Troubled by Interdisciplinarity? *Science*, April 6.

Platt, J. 1981. On Interviewing One's Peers. *British Journal of Sociology* 32 (1): 75–91.

Rhoten, Diana. 2004. Interdisciplinary Research: Trend or Transition. *Items and Issues* 5 (1–2): 6–11.

Rylance, Rick. 2015. Global Funders to Focus on Interdisciplinarity. *Nature* 525: 313–315.

Sá, Creso M. 2008. 'Interdisciplinary Strategies' in U.S. Research Universities. *Higher Education* 55: 537–552.

Schön, Donald. 1983. *The Reflective Practitioner: How Professionals Think in Action.* London: Maurice Temple Smith.

Slow Science Academy. 2010. The Slow Science Manifesto. http://slow-science. org. Accessed 24 January 2019.

Sperber, D. 2003. Why Rethink Interdisciplinarity?. Presentation for the Virtual Seminar, Rethinking Interdisciplinarity (2004, February), www.dan.sperber. fr/?p=101. Accessed 24/1/19.

Szostak, R. 2015. Interdisciplinarity: Resources Abound (Letter to Nature). *Nature* 526: 506.

UKRI. 2018. Strategic Prospectus: Building the UKRI Strategy. www.ukri.org/files/about/ukri-strategy-document-pdf/?pdf=Strategic-Prospectus. Accessed 24/1/19.

van der Zwaan, Bert. 2017. *Higher Education in 2040. A Global Approach.* Amsterdam: Amsterdam University Press.

Vienni, B., P. Cruz, L. Repetto, C. von Sanden, A. Lorieto, and V. Fernández, eds. 2015. *Encuentros sobre Interdisciplina.* Montevideo: Espacio Interdisciplinario de la Universidad de la Republica.

Weingart, Peter. 2000. Interdisciplinarity: The Paradoxical Discourse. In *Practising Interdisciplinarity*, ed. Peter Weingart and Nico Stehr, 25–41. Toronto: University of Toronto Press.

Weingart, P. 2014. Interdisciplinarity and the New Governance of Universities. In *University Experiments in Interdisciplinarity: Obstacles and Opportunities*, ed. P. Weingart and B. Padberg. Bielefeld: Transcript Verlag.

Woelert, Peter. 2015. Governing Knowledge: The Formalization Dilemma in the Governance of the Public Sciences. *Minerva* 53 (1): 1–19.

Woelert, Peter, and Victoria Millar. 2013. The 'Paradox of Interdisciplinarity' in Australian Research Governance. *Higher Education* 66: 755–767.

CHAPTER 2

"What Am I?" The Path to Becoming an Interdisciplinary Academic

In 1999 two of the UK Research Councils came together to launch the joint Economic and Social Research Council/Natural Environment Research Council Interdisciplinary Research Studentships. Their goal was to promote greater interaction between the social and environmental sciences and to help generate a community of professional researchers capable of working across these sets of disciplines. Between 1999 and 2004 the scheme awarded some 123 PhD studentships, representing a total investment approaching £3.5 million (Meagher and Lyall 2005).

Five years later, in 2004, the Economic and Social Research Council and the Medical Research Council introduced the Interdisciplinary Research Studentship and Post-Doctoral Fellowship Scheme, with the intention of supporting both postgraduate students wishing to study for a PhD qualification in the social and medical sciences and early career researchers (ECRs) who had recently completed their PhD. As with the ESRC/NERC studentship scheme, the main objective was to allow applicants to develop new research skills while tackling projects that were genuinely interdisciplinary in nature. It was also intended that this scheme would promote greater interaction between the social and medical sciences, and lead to the development of a body of professional social and medical scientists. ESRC/MRC jointly awarded up to 20 studentships and

© The Author(s) 2019
C. Lyall, *Being an Interdisciplinary Academic*,
https://doi.org/10.1007/978-3-030-18659-3_2

10 post-doctoral fellowships[1] under this scheme each year; 82 studentships and 32 post-doctoral fellowships had been awarded, representing an investment of about £2.4 million each year, by the time we were commissioned to evaluate the scheme in 2009 (Meagher and Lyall 2009).

I was part of the team that conducted independent evaluations of both of these schemes, commissioned by ESRC to provide the funders with a sound evidence base with which to assess the future of these schemes and to consider applicability of the model elsewhere. These evaluation reports (Meagher and Lyall 2005, 2009) assessed micro issues related to the operation of the funding schemes and macro issues related to the changing academic landscape for interdisciplinary research.

In both cases, our evaluations strongly supported the continuation of the funding schemes, due to their perceived success and to the absence of other opportunities for interdisciplinary postgraduate training in the UK at that time.[2] While our informants in both studies showed great enthusiasm for the intellectual benefits conferred by interdisciplinary research, views were more mixed, or qualified, regarding the extent to which interdisciplinary work was an advantage in career development. In both reports (ibid.) we therefore suggested that if Research Councils genuinely wished to see interdisciplinary research as part of the UK's academic landscape, then it was imperative that they facilitate career paths for interdisciplinary researchers, ensuring that they were not disadvantaged by existing governance structures.

Among the governance issues that we highlighted (ibid. 2005, p. 3) was what we termed "institutional departmentalism" as well as the limitations of the, then, Research Assessment Exercise (RAE),[3] and indeed the operation of the Research Councils' own administrative processes at that time. We considered that all of these aspects worked against academic employment prospects, placing constraints on future academic career paths for students undertaking interdisciplinary PhDs although we also expressed hope that academia was slowly evolving towards greater acceptance of such types of careers.

[1] A key change from the earlier ESRC/NERC scheme was that, this time, the Research Councils were offering a two-year interdisciplinary post-doctoral fellowship as well as the PhD studentship.

[2] These funding schemes no longer exist and have been replaced by the Doctoral Training Centre model: see Filippakopoulou (2017) for a further explanation of this funding model and www.ukri.org/skills/funding-for-research-training (accessed 17/12/18).

[3] See Chap. 3 for a further discussion of the RAE and its replacement, the REF.

Our 2005 survey respondents (supervisors and students) were generally optimistic that the interdisciplinary nature of the ESRC/NERC studentship would enhance students' employability and nearly two-thirds of supervisors disagreed that in the future interdisciplinary training could be seen as a disadvantage in academia. In 2009, the majority of student awardholders and supervisors/mentors (80% and 84% respectively) felt that engaging in interdisciplinary research leads to significant career benefits for ECRs but a notable fraction (19%) of supervisors/mentors agreed that interdisciplinary research leads to considerable career *disincentives* for ECRs.

Focus group discussions with a sample of supervisors in 2005 flagged serious constraints on academic career paths for interdisciplinary students. These participants noted that, even those students whose innovative interdisciplinary work was received well at conferences, for example, could feel that they were disadvantaged when prospective university employers prioritise ability to teach in a discipline (an issue that still persists today as discussed in Chap. 3). Similarly, in one-to-one interviews, only a handful of supervisors were wholly positive about the interdisciplinary studentship contributing to academic employment, and some had mixed feelings, with many voicing real concerns about employment prospects in "tribal" academia. While students who discussed employability in these interviews appeared to be fairly optimistic that they would be prepared to take advantage of such changes in academia, our 2005 report notes that these students frequently used the word "hope". Students in our 2005 focus group were frustrated by the feeling that they needed to be in a single discipline to get jobs: "Going wide in your PhD is what seems right, then there is the feeling that academia wants you to narrow" (Meagher and Lyall 2005, p. 39).

Although acknowledging that fundamental transformation would take longer, our focus group participants in 2005 expected the academic landscape to change in the next 15 years. They saw this coming about in great part through the efforts of currently established academics who have, themselves, "travelled the journey" to interdisciplinarity.

The holders of both the ESRC/MRC and the ESRC/NERC awards were seen to be at least as strong intellectually as conventional postgraduate studentship awardholders and both schemes were perceived as affording otherwise unavailable opportunities to undertake innovative, interdisciplinary types of projects. Both schemes were rated very highly by those involved, with wide support for their continuation. In our evaluators' conclusions we noted that the ESRC/MRC interdisciplinary funding scheme was building capacity by generating high-calibre individuals who were capable of continuing to undertake interdisciplinary research in areas of potential interest to both the Research Councils involved but we cautioned:

> Whether or not the academic context of the future allows or encourages them to do so remains to be seen. (Meagher and Lyall 2009, p. 45)

This then provides the starting point for my career history interviews with previous awardholders of these studentships, the most senior of whom were 15 years post PhD at the time of interviewing. During these conversations we discussed how their careers as academics had actually developed and whether the academic landscape for interdisciplinary research—and employment prospects—have indeed changed. Various themes emerged that underpin the continuing narrative in the chapters that follow, including our sense of academic "identity", what it means to have a successful academic career, and the role that serendipity might play in this.

MOTIVATIONS

I started each interview by asking informants to talk about their motivations for undertaking a purposely interdisciplinary PhD. A recurrent theme was a coincidence of circumstances, rather than the applicant specifically setting out to do a piece of interdisciplinary research and then actively seeking a suitable studentship. Supervisors were influential in suggesting these joint studentships as potential sources of funding and luck or "opportunism" also played a part, for example:

> [T]o be perfectly frank, it was purely opportunistic…it just sort of happened really. (Diana)

Practical considerations certainly had a role in the form of achievable funding deadlines or the added kudos of a better-funded studentship. But others had been more explicit in seeking out an interdisciplinary approach, either because of the research they wanted to do and a realisation that this required disciplinary transition, or because of the profession they wanted to pursue, or previous exposure to this approach at the undergraduate level, or indeed because of personal temperament:

> [I couldn't] really envisage doing any other type of PhD. (Iona)

When discussing their motivations for undertaking an interdisciplinary PhD, my informants fell into three groups. First, there were those who were influenced either by prior education and training (e.g. Helena, Iona, Louisa, Tristan, Vera) or who had already identified their own research topics (e.g. Carina, Fiona, Gina) so this group was dedicated to pursuing interdisciplinary research from the outset of their postgraduate journey.

There was then a second group who were, to an extent, sensitised to interdisciplinarity via their undergraduate geography degrees that encompassed both social and physical elements and who were then influenced by their supervisors to follow a more interdisciplinary postgraduate path (e.g. Norman, Owen and Quentin).

Finally, there is the group whom I have termed "opportunistic" as in "this opportunity cropped up" as Paterson, along with others explained, that would-be supervisors guided them towards the joint studentship opportunities.[4] In many respects, it is this group that is of greatest interest because I will link them to a later discussion about the role of serendipity in interdisciplinary research when I ask how, in our modern, metric-driven academic lives, do we retain space for chance and opportunism, which are arguably the lifeblood of scholarly creativity?

Tristan's relatively rapid career trajectory prompted me to consider whether there might be a link between high achievers being more strategic in their career choices whereas others may have had a tendency to simply drift into interdisciplinary research because the opportunity presented itself. I wondered if there might be a link between the people who move institutions versus the ones who stay, those who actively pursue an interdisciplinary career or those who are content to let things happen to them? However, interrogating the interview data did not reveal any obvious links between any demographic features, such as level of seniority and whether the informant had moved from their PhD host institution (see Appendix B). In any case, the nature of this research design did not present a meaningful sample that would permit this type of rigorous correlation.

It was, however, notable that interviewees did tend to describe taking advantage of a situation rather than actively seeking interdisciplinary research opportunities. I expected to hear that they had approached their

---

[4] Many PhD topics are shaped by the supervisor and, indeed in the natural sciences, it is customary for the supervisor to present the student with the research question. One would also expect potential supervisors to advise applicants on potential sources of funding so we cannot infer too much from the fact that many informants talked about the influence of their supervisor as part of the motivation for starting down this interdisciplinary route.

careers in a more planned way rather than essentially happenstance. So how do these interviewees actually symbolise what I have termed "opportunism", simply that they were taking advantage of an open funding call? How might their careers have evolved had these studentship schemes not been available to them?

Katya goes some way to answering these conjectures: as a medical sociologist based in a sociology department who, by her own admission, was not a high flyer, her department would not have nominated her for one of their allocated ESRC awards. Mariana also expressed the view that she would not have been competitive enough for a single discipline award from ESRC because her degree in biology would preclude her from gaining a pure social science studentship. This then raises the question of quality: might one infer that the interdisciplinary schemes were seen as accepting "second best" candidates who were not good enough for the single discipline competitions? This imputation is firmly negated by the findings of our evaluations of these schemes (Meagher and Lyall 2005, 2009) where the graduates of these awards were deemed by their supervisors to be "at least as good" as other PhD students whom they had supervised. An alternative interpretation could be that these interdisciplinary studentship schemes were more willing to take a gamble and to fund projects and perhaps candidates who were seen as "intellectual risk takers" (Augsburg 2014).

As discussed in Chap. 1, interdisciplinarity takes many forms and this can influence the types of career paths that academic researchers experience. In a previous study (Lyall et al. 2011) we identified, using the Q sort method, two groups ("factors") of interdisciplinary researchers and developed the following characterisations for the two factors, which illustrate different motivations for interdisciplinarity.

One group ("Problem solvers") was focused on the role of interdisciplinarity in solving problems. The standpoint captured by this factor emphasises interdisciplinary approaches as a way of addressing real-world problems which will also provide research that better serves the needs of the economy and promotes application of research in policy and practice. Interdisciplinary research is underpinned by synthesising and integrating research output and by working together to find things out. Discipline experts, working in collaboration with other researchers from different disciplines, typically carry out this form of interdisciplinary research.

The second group, which we termed "Individual careers", was focused on the role of interdisciplinarity in the context of their own careers. This factor agrees with the "Problem solvers" that the real world is not divided up by academic disciplines. However, the focus of working with researchers from other disciplines is the context of broadening horizons and improving the individual's own research. Different disciplines offer more than just different perspectives as they can also confront ingrained assumptions.

Although the interviewees in the current sample might span both archetypes, the nature of their graduate training meant that they more frequently fell into the category of "Individual careers".

Career Aspirations and Development

Having started by talking about their motivation for undertaking an interdisciplinary PhD, I then asked awardholders what their aspirations had been for their career at that stage when they were just starting out on their graduate studies. We then moved the conversation on to talking about how their career had developed, if indeed it had developed how they had hoped, and whether they had had any particular career development strategies.

Responses to the question about career aspirations again fell broadly into three groups:

1. those who had no career plans while doing their PhD: "Honestly? I didn't have the foggiest clue" (Norman)
2. those who wanted to stay in academia or at least wanted to be a university researcher (Katya and Una, for example, were adamant that they did not want teaching roles and this theme of research-only careers is explored further in Chap. 3)
3. and a comparably sized group of people who wanted to continue to do research but were not certain that it had to be in an academic role, reflecting previous experiences with NGOs or consultancy firms

My introductory email had allowed for the fact that the awardholders whom I was inviting for interview may no longer consider that they were working in an interdisciplinary way, despite the earlier focus of their PhD. So when I asked if interdisciplinarity still featured in their current role the responses ranged from a definite "yes" to something more equivocal. None of my respondents had abandoned their interdisciplinary roots completely but for some it was a question of degree, perhaps reflecting the fact that respondents were now in lectureships where teaching took up more of their time. Norman ascribed this to the "institutional set up" within his current department and partly to the fact that "research career trajectories change over time". This mixed picture was also presented by another geographer who noted that it had been useful to him to be able to show that he could work across the "gaps between different specialisms" (Owen) but went on to acknowledge that many aspects of his day-to-day activities (teaching and research) were "still quite disciplinary".

I asked informants if they could say if their career had unfolded as they expected and, if necessary, prompted them with the question "are you where you expected to be in your career by now?". Career progression had been reasonably straightforward for Diana, Owen and Quentin, and Reuben admitted to his career developing "Probably better than I expected". In contrast, when I interviewed her, Selina was about to give up her academic career and retrain in another profession. Others too recognised that they were taking a harder route: Helena, who was someone straddling academic and professional roles, did wonder "why am I making life hard for myself", acknowledging that "it would be so much easier if I just did what is the more defined pathway" but she answered her own question with this:

> [T]he reason I'm doing what I'm doing and meshing it together is because that's what I really enjoy, and not only enjoy, I think that's what's beneficial to the NHS. So it does take a bit longer, and it's a bit more of a meandering road. (Helena)

Achieving various conventional academic career milestones, such as external awards and fellowships and reaching senior grades, were not guarantors of a sense of personal success. Louisa was concerned that publications had not been "that great" and she worried about her "real limitations as an academic" saying that she "certainly [wouldn't] have a stellar career". Was this female modesty rather than anything to do with interdisciplinarity or are interdisciplinary researchers actually less confident about their academic status?

Interviewees drew comparisons with the progress of their monodisciplinary colleagues. Belinda, who was eight years post PhD, was finding promotion difficult in her department because of the nature of her research and, specifically, the different publication rates of qualitative and quantitative researchers which she believed led to a lack of parity in promotion prospects. Fiona (nine years post PhD) portrayed her recent promotion to

Senior Lecturer as "not easy to come by" and described how, in comparison with her monodisciplinary peers, both her interdisciplinary background and the fact that she had moved between different countries had held her back.

Women in the sample had made career choices that had involved maternity leaves and part-time working (not, of course, choices that are solely the preserve of interdisciplinary academics). Carina clearly felt that her maternity leaves had delayed her promotion to Senior Lecturer as she talked about the well-meaning but patronising attitudes of senior (male) colleagues (again, sadly not unique to the interdisciplinary world). Even for those who did appear to have been more strategic, with a clearer idea of what was required for progression, acknowledged "massive challenges":

> At every point there are challenges ... the structures in the university don't fully understand it... So you spend a lot of your time explaining ...what you're trying to do, what the importance and the benefits of that are, to a whole range of people who will often say "yes, we're completely committed", but then when it comes to sign on the dotted line, that's when it gets even trickier. (Helena)

Yet few interviewees were willing to admit to having had any career strategy and reflected a lack of planning in the early stages: "When I was young I would go more on the basis of enjoying what I'm doing now" (Carina). Similarly, Diana admitted "without really planning it, I have had an interdisciplinary trajectory" while Erica used the very telling phrase "I just jog along and see what happens". Quentin "didn't really have any expectations" and described how

> through no real planning or strategy on my part, I've ended up with some quite marketable skills ... I've never had a specific career strategy. It's literally—I'll be honest—the one I came up with when I did my Masters which was, if someone is willing to pay me, I'll stay in university—is pretty much still my main guiding strategy but I guess there's a corollary to it which is, if it's still interesting. (Quentin)

This theme of doing things that people enjoyed or found interesting was widespread, even if that came at the expense of career progression. Fiona was not alone in admitting to being casual about her career and lacking purpose ("I've had different kind of goal posts") but acknowledged that it had not necessarily served her well. Mariana, who had had a varied career as a policy researcher for a global organisation and as a research administrator before returning to academic research, was someone else who had "no expectations actually for my career". Norman also acknowledged that his career had not developed as he thought it might but he was relaxed about this:

> I'm not particularly careerist in that sense, so I don't have ambitions to be a young professor or anything like that. So that kind of slowness and perhaps that slight slowness in publications and in promotions or something like that really just doesn't worry me and I know that's distinct to me rather than (LAUGHS)—not everyone else would feel the same about that. But that doesn't worry me.[5] (Norman)

This prompted me to wonder whether all academics are simply reluctant to present themselves in interviews as too "careerist" or too driven and whether I would have received similar responses had I interviewed academic colleagues who had pursued more traditional academic careers?

External pressures inevitably influence career choices, for example, Diana's account of how her career had developed described how, when she joined her current department, she had felt compelled to conform to its biological (rather than social) research focus. Partly through career progression, Diana had then been able to move back towards the social sciences but this had not been a seamless process:

> [N]ow it feels like I can write a story and it all looks beautifully linear and flowing from one thing to the next, but it wasn't like that at all. (Diana)

This ideal of the "career narrative" was echoed by others:

- Quentin spoke about "retrofitting" his career to fit promotion expectations
- Helena described how the fellowship application she was writing was helping her to "make sense of her journey" and talked about the importance of identifying one's "research golden thread"
- Fiona recollected similar advice from her PhD supervisor about the importance of developing her own "niche" but found it difficult to write a "coherent story" about her contributions to knowledge as a social scientist

---

[5] This observation from Norman introduces the idea of "slowness" which is explored further in conjunction with the question about how we facilitate serendipity within the modern academy in Chap. 5.

As interdisciplinary researchers, do we retrospectively construct our career so that it looks planned and seamless as these interviewees suggest? Perhaps it takes more time to be able to look back on an interdisciplinary career and identify—and then hold on to—Helena's "golden thread". Nevertheless, these seem to be key tactics in the development of a successful interdisciplinary career and form the crux of the argument that will be presented in Chap. 4 on the implications for academic capacity building.

Ultimately, having a career "strategy" may not be an option in the current academic climate. Katya was in the depressing situation of working on short, three-month contracts and would "literally work on anything if it gives me a job". Career decisions may therefore be simply pragmatic:

> [I]t was a full-time position for three years. You don't really turn that down do you? (Belinda)

Nevertheless, the idea of being lucky or fortunate in one's career and the role played by chance were recurring themes in these conversations; Vera was not the only interviewee who used the term "serendipitous" when talking about her career development.

Awardholders, as we saw above, were also admitting to not having an overt career strategy or a particularly clear motivation for starting out on an interdisciplinary career. It may be that academics who follow an interdisciplinary route need to be more flexible in their careers and are less able to follow a pre-defined path. This has implications for leadership at the departmental and institutional levels and also for the broader governance environment with respect to the funding landscape so, in Chap. 6, I discuss what might be appropriate roles for institutions in supporting and facilitating interdisciplinary careers.

Career Highs and Lows

I asked awardholders if they could talk about some of their career highs and lows.[6] This "career high" question provoked a number of responses (see Table 2.1) that would represent conventional career milestones for any academic without, necessarily, being particular to interdisciplinarity unless, of course, one shares the opinion, supported by a substantial body of literature (e.g. Castán Broto et al. 2009; Evans and Randalls 2008;

---

[6] If necessary, I followed this up with prompts such as "what has helped to move your career forward?" or "what do you think has held you back?"

Table 2.1   Career highs

Getting the PhD (Belinda, Helena)
Getting a postdoc fellowship (Carina)
Being awarded personal fellowships (Diana)
The lab in which she worked being awarded a national prize (Erica)
Being a collaborator in projects funded by an interdisciplinary programme that enabled
her to develop her geographical scope (Gina)
The privilege of doing a PhD and devoting three years to her own work (Helena)
Getting on to a professional training scheme (Helena)
Getting a large grant and setting up her own team (Julia)
Getting a paper from PhD published (Katya)
First publication (Paterson)
Career milestones: Postdoc, lectureship (Paterson)
Specific published article, large grant (Quentin)
Having papers published in high-impact journals (Iona, Reuben)
Getting prestigious grants (Reuben, Gina)
Setting up a new research group (Tristan)
Career development fellowship (Una)

Golde and Gallagher 1999; Zucker 2012), that would say that it might be harder for interdisciplinarians to achieve these goals.

Others were more reflective about what it meant to be interdisciplinary and linked their career highs to that. For example, pride in outputs from a very interdisciplinary collaboration or seeing a long-term project come to fruition:

> [T]hat paper kind of encapsulated kind of just a really important way in which … people with different perspectives could come together and critically engage with a concept like [topic] and that we were able to bring all of our different ideas together and work together to produce something. (Norman)

> [T]he high is then when you do later on realise—well, actually, yeah, look at this paper that we wrote, who would have thought that three years ago when we had only just met one another … that we would have been able to get to this point. They're the high points. (Owen)

Tristan identified success in carving out a role for social science in a department dominated by the natural sciences. These three responses encapsulate the purpose and thrill of interdisciplinary research, despite the challenges, but not everyone shared these views:

Table 2.2 Career lows

Impact of maternity leave on career progression (Carina, Katya)
A grant application blocked because it did not fit with the unit's strategy (Diana)
The struggle to complete PhD thesis due to family issues (Erica)
Issues with employment contracts (Fiona, Julia, Una)
Poor supervision (Katya, Mariana)
The struggle to find a postdoc position (Louisa)
Workload management, especially as a new lecturer (Owen)
Dispiriting paper and grant rejections (Paterson, Selina)

[I]t's quite hard to sort of get a buzz from research that takes a long time to come to fruition and then a long time to either get appreciated or not. (Paterson)

Again, when it came to talking about career lows, there was a spectrum of responses (see Table 2.2) and some career lows were not, on the face of it, problems unique to interdisciplinarity as one could argue that all academics, regardless of discipline, might face these obstacles. However, given what we know about the well-rehearsed tribulations of interdisciplinary research, it is not a stretch to consider that these matters may have been exacerbated by the interdisciplinary context in which respondents found themselves.

Other career lows were much more clearly attributable to the interdisciplinary nature of their work, such as feeling ill equipped and out of one's depth or the wearisomeness of constant self-justification:

[I]t was just incredibly difficult and not even vaguely what I wanted to be doing...It was awful being an anthropologist thrown into that, and really at quite a junior level, first job postdoc and not getting a huge deal of support...not being able to develop your skills. By the end of it I felt completely de-skilled. (Belinda)

[T]he groundwork that needs doing is energy-sapping, and also time-sapping. Whilst I'm trying to write the content of what a fellowship is, I'm also doing all of this groundwork to explain who I am to loads of people, to make the case for why the work is important ... that can be overwhelming in terms of the amount of time that takes to do, and often does make me think should I just give up. (Helena)

KEY TURNING POINTS

In conjunction with the question about career highs and lows, interviewees were asked if they could describe any key turning points in their career. These might have been paths not taken, for example, a deliberate decision not to be "the token geographer in an engineering department" (Owen). Paradigmatic shifts were key: moving from an anthropology department to a medical school presented Belinda with a theoretical turning point, moving from an interpretivist tradition to a positivist one where she had to learn to hold her ground theoretically in this new environment. Reuben's move, essentially in the opposite direction from biology to anthropology, and being exposed to different disciplinary approaches and traditions was similarly "an eye opener".

More conventionally, Diana's turning point was getting her first Principal Investigator (PI) role although, what was significant for an interdisciplinarian in a medical-led department, was that it then enabled her to shape her own research direction counter to the prevailing medical culture. But the grant application process could be much less positive. In a scenario that all academic researchers, regardless of discipline, may be all too familiar with, Selina spoke about an unsuccessful fellowship application as "the beginning of the end" of her career as an academic:

> I hated the whole experience, it knocked me back quite a lot with my enthusiasm for my work generally (LAUGHS) and then I just thought, actually, this is what an academic career is, you know, I'm going to have to be doing this day in, day out really and I don't like it. (Selina)

Chance meetings, cited as key turning points, again highlight the role that serendipity has played in these careers. Quentin was particularly clear about the role that chance had played at key points in his career. We turn to the vexing—and perhaps unanswerable question—of how institutions might facilitate such serendipitous encounters in Chap. 5.

SENSE OF IDENTITY

So where did this process of "becoming interdisciplinary" leave my interviewees; how do they now describe themselves as academics? I discussed this issue of identity with each of my awardholder interviewees, using

Table 2.3 Questions to prompt reflections on interdisciplinary identity

Are you a discipline specialist working in interdisciplinary research projects?
Are you a researcher with multiple skills and able to draw on several disciplines?
Does your research focus on only one discipline?
What label do you use to introduce yourself, for example, "I am a sociologist"?
Do you describe yourself in another way?
Do you describe yourself differently depending on the context?

various prompts and suggestions (see Table 2.3). An interdisciplinary identity may be seen to lack the prestige of a discipline-focused academic and can be perceived as risky and outside the norm (Cuevas-Garcia 2015), rendering such individuals "academic nomads without a tribe" (Tait 1999). They may be less confident about their identity as scholars and feel that they risk being considered "amateurs" by their monodisciplinary peers. These interdisciplinarians may also need to assume multiple and shifting identities (Lingard et al. 2016).

This sense of identity was firmly related to maintaining academic status. Carina recognised that women such as herself, who had had more than one period of maternity leave, often ended up losing their sense of a scholarly identity as a result of "scatter gunning" (working on lots of different projects) and had thought carefully about her own "brand":

I decided to establish my identity as a medical sociologist, and that's what I was going to introduce myself as ... I wanted to be a "something". (Carina)

This process of deliberation about one's academic identity and having a suitable "label" was a shared concern. Una described herself as a specialist in a particular technique but wanted to carve out her own research identity as "a good public health researcher", not wanting to be seen as "just a technician", while Mariana had looked at the websites of others working in a similar field to understand how they described themselves in order to answer her question:

[W]hat am I?... because if you say you're an interdisciplinary scientist, what does that mean? (Mariana)

This process of becoming an interdisciplinary academic could also be about a loss of identity: Katya felt like "I'm losing the sociologist in us

[sic] which is a bit of a shame" while Belinda had stopped describing herself as an anthropologist and no longer identified with a particular discipline or methodology.

This description of self was something that could emerge over time:

> I'm a health geographer but …it's taken quite a long time to reach a point where I feel like I can say that and to decide, yes, that is what I'm going to call myself and it's been a conscious decision to choose that label. (Selina)

Selina had settled on "health geographer" because she had an eye to future careers and needed to have an identity "to help me frame myself", suggesting that one needs a recognisable label in order to conform to academic norms where disciplinary connections prevail:

> I view myself as having a home discipline and a home working culture and set of theories and methods but then feel able to draw on other disciplines, either through my own work or collaboratively as well. But I think having that sense of home is quite important to me. (Diana)

Universities are still more comfortable with traditional career trajectories (see also Chap. 6) and labels came more readily to some; Erica, for example, was quite clear about being a medical anthropologist, and descriptions of self were more straightforward for those who identified with geography, either as a parent department or as their original degree subject. Paterson was unusual among the sample of awardholders in labelling himself as a "disciplinary expert" at psychology and described himself as a psychologist who would draw on the expertise of others as required.

Respondents addressed this identity issue in tactical ways, for example, using "inside" and "outside" labels to maintain coherence within a department:

> This is almost by agreement, some others of us who are interdisciplinary, when we talk to our colleagues in the department we refer to ourselves as human geographers, but when I'm outside of those circles I'm an environmental social scientist. (Fiona)

or for diplomatic reasons: Gina chose to identify with her undergraduate ecology degree "as an excuse for poor understanding of social science" or in order to identify with other ecologists so that she does not appear to be "like a sociologist that's attacking them without understanding what they're trying to do" (Gina). Julia typically eschewed the term "interdisciplinary" to describe herself, "unless writing a grant application in which case I say it 20,000 times".

This theme of flexible identities was widespread and respondents talked about repackaging themselves depending on the context. When I asked Norman how he felt about having this rather malleable academic identity his response was an immediate "I love it". But others found their academic identity much less straightforward. Helena described herself as "a perpetual fence-sitter". The emphasis on the applied nature of her work was critical for Helena but the fact that she held a dual appointment and consequently had multiple identities (resulting in five different email accounts) was stressful:

> It's all me but which bit of me... this trying to explain yourself to everyone just gets so overwhelming. (Helena)

Tactics to get round this "identity crisis" included focusing on topic areas rather than discipline (Anna), but insecurity and identity fatigue were features of interdisciplinary careers:

> [I]t's easier [to describe herself as an anthropologist] ... you know, it's always a bit tiring to go into endless detail ... I also like anthropology ... I just feel I'm not maybe the best person to represent it. (Louisa)

Reuben tried to reject labels:

> This is something I always struggle with because I really don't like those labels. Well, I certainly don't fit easily into them ... I always like to be question-driven or problem driven, be looking at what's the thing in the world that I want to understand and try to explain. When push comes to shove, I use phrases like human evolutionary ecologist. (Reuben)

But the lack of a convenient label also makes other people very insecure:

> [T]hey find it problematic when you don't have a discipline. (Gina)

This chapter has assessed some of the areas of commonality and difference that interviewees presented for their reasons for following an interdisciplinary career path and the routes they had taken, noting some of the milestones that they had passed along the way. It has also reflected on some of the destinations that they have reached regarding their professional identities. Significantly, Reuben's phrase "when push comes to shove" hints at the fact that, as academics, we cannot escape labels. I develop this theme further in later chapters when I discuss the pervasive notion of the traditional academic and uncertainties about identity in relation to teaching roles. But first we move on to examine how interviewees judged the impact of their institutions on their interdisciplinary careers.

Talking Points
A group of academics whose doctoral studies were explicitly interdisciplinary have spoken about their career motivations and aspirations, and the challenges and opportunities that they have faced, reflecting on their sense of academic identity as interdisciplinarians and the consequences this has for their status in the academy.

Is interdisciplinary research a risky choice within the context of academic careers? Is this changing with the increasing popularity of this style of working within our universities? What could be done at personal, local and national levels to provide more consistent messages to young (and not so young) researchers about how, when and indeed whether to follow this route?

REFERENCES

Augsburg, Tanya. 2014. Becoming Transdisciplinary: The Emergence of the Transdisciplinary Individual. *World Futures* 70 (3–4): 233–247.

Castán Broto, Vanesa, Maya Gislason, and Melf-Hinrich Ehlers. 2009. Practising Interdisciplinarity in the Interplay Between Disciplines: Experiences of Established Researchers. *Environmental Science & Policy* 12 (7): 922–933.

Cuevas-Garcia, C.A. 2015. 'I Have Never Cared for Particular Disciplines' – Negotiating an Interdisciplinary Self in Biographical Narrative. *Contemporary Social Science* 10 (1): 86–98.

Evans, James, and Samuel Randalls. 2008. Geography and Paratactical Interdisciplinarity: Views from the ESRC–NERC PhD Studentship Programme. *Geoforum* 39 (2): 581–592.

Filippakopoulou, Maria. 2017. The Shift Towards Doctoral Training Partnerships in the United Kingdom Higher Education: The BBSRC DTP Governance Model – Potential and Impact. Master's dissertation, University of Edinburgh.

Golde, Chris M., and Hanna Alix Gallagher. 1999. The Challenges of Conducting Interdisciplinary Research in Traditional Doctoral Programs. *Ecosystems* 2: 281–285.

Lingard, Lorelei, Catherine F. Schryer, Marlee M. Spafford, and Sandra L. Campbell. 2016. Negotiating the Politics of Identity in an Interdisciplinary Research Team. *Qualitative Research* 7 (4): 501–519.

Lyall, C., A. Bruce, W. Marsden, and L. Meagher. 2011. Identifying Key Success Factors in the Quest for Interdisciplinary Knowledge. Report to NERC.

Meagher, Laura, and Catherine Lyall. 2005. Evaluation of the ESRC/NERC Interdisciplinary Research Studentship Scheme. Report to ESRC.

———. 2009. Evaluation of ESRC/MRC Interdisciplinary Research Studentship and Post-Doctoral Fellowship Scheme. Report to ESRC.

Tait, J. 1999. Help for the Academic Nomads in Search of Their Own Sympathetic Tribe. *Times Higher Education*, March 5.

Zucker, D. 2012. Developing Your Career in an Age of Team Science. *Journal of Investigative Medicine* 60 (5): 779–784.

CHAPTER 3

"Are You One of Us?" How Institutions Impact Interdisciplinary Careers

THE FUNDING DRIVER

Interdisciplinarity has become "a master steering mechanism in government science policy" (Lowe and Phillipson 2006) yet, there is an incongruity in institutions championing interdisciplinarity through the award of competitive interdisciplinary studentships, for example, "while not changing the conventions that make it so difficult for those who choose this route early in their careers to actually progress" (Bryne 2014). Individuals pursuing interdisciplinary careers do not do so in a vacuum; their career opportunities and obstacles are rooted in, and deeply affected by, their particular institutional context. National and international funding and quality assessment regimes are also part of this "institutional ecosystem", along with the institutional tactics implemented by universities in response, which can also have significant impacts on academic careers.[1]

Awardholders underscored how widely interdisciplinarity featured in public funding programmes ("try and find a call that doesn't have interdisciplinarity … somewhere in the lingo", Tristan), openly acknowledging the influence that the availability of such funding had on personal interdisciplinary research programmes:

---

[1] This broad "institutional ecosystem" is variously populated by members of promotion committees, heads of departments, deans and vice rectors of universities, and university REF co-ordinators but also journal editors, grant reviewers, and learned academies and professional groups, as well as the staff within those agencies that fund and assess research quality.

© The Author(s) 2019
C. Lyall, *Being an Interdisciplinary Academic*,
https://doi.org/10.1007/978-3-030-18659-3_3

[W]e all, to a greater or lesser degree, make strategic decisions about which directions we're going in based on what money's out there and what's not. (Diana)

This funding focus is reinforced by data from the ESRC, which show that 70% of ESRC grants are "in some sense multidisciplinary" and "more than a quarter of ESRC grants extend into disciplines outside ESRC's remit" (ESRC n.d.; see also Hulkes 2018). Nonetheless, apprehensions were expressed (e.g. Gina, Iona and Julia) about the undue influence that "following the money" had on universities' research strategies:

I think they're just pressured by money, they're influenced by where they can get the money from, it's not necessarily a belief in the good that interdisciplinary research can do, which a lot of interdisciplinary researchers have. (Gina)

The "Global Challenges Research Fund" (GCRF)[2] was a particular case in point at the time of interviewing, with research leaders citing this as a key motivator for large-scale, interdisciplinary collaborative research grant applications from across their institutions. Nevertheless, the timescales for such complex collaborative bids were a concern for research leaders who noted the time it takes to mobilise the community to respond to a call (VR1) and the need for longer funding commitments in order to justify establishing costly and time-consuming overseas relationships (VR2).

This played into wider observations about the funding horizons of interdisciplinary research. Echoing Abbott (2001), concerns were voiced about universities undertaking problem-focused research that was "à la mode" but might not be resilient (VR1). While the establishment of UK Research and Innovation (UKRI) was generally taken as a signal that there would be a continuing emphasis on interdisciplinarity, SR3 acknowledged that there was uncertainty about the future balance between cross-council challenge led funding (such as GCRF) and the funding to the disciplines via the individual research councils. Failing to maintain the momentum that interdisciplinary research had gained within research policy would be problematic for those academics who had been encouraged to pursue an interdisciplinary career. Far safer, perhaps, to be a discipline-based expert

[2] https://www.ukri.org/research/global-challenges-research-fund (accessed 19/12/18).

who can collaborate in an interdisciplinary[3] team with the option of retreating back to the security of one's own discipline, if the fashion for funding interdisciplinary research were to wane, rather than risk pursuing a truly interdisciplinary career? This was certainly the underlying view of some university leaders, as I discuss in Chap. 4.

CHANGES TO THE INTERDISCIPLINARY LANDSCAPE

Given these UK funding trends,[4] I asked awardholders if they had seen changes in the way that interdisciplinarity was treated over the course of their career, either within the micro-environment of their own university or within the macro-environment of the broader research community.

This revealed a general difference of opinion among awardholders although more considered interdisciplinarity to be on the increase, using terms such as "professionalised" and "formalised" to describe interdisciplinary research practice within their institutions. However, Norman was not the only interviewee to say that interdisciplinarity was not encouraged as much now as it used to be. Partly he ascribed this to the work pressures of his lectureship, which had dampened his ability to do interdisciplinary research in contrast to his post-doctoral experience, but he also attributed this decline to the increasing focus on "delivery" which is a theme that we pick up again in Chap. 5.

A similar disparity was expressed when we discussed whether interdisciplinary research was now more "mainstream": VR3 described it as "baked in" to her[5] university's research strategy, Tristan used the term "hard-wired" and Selina said she heard the word less but ascribed this to it having become more embedded and no longer a novelty. Quentin declared that it was pervasive in all forms of research but did draw a distinction between the teaching and research contexts for interdisciplinarity: in the case of the former "people are still trying to crack that nut" but in the research world, it had gone from "a niche thing to mainstream …

---

[3] Or perhaps, more accurately, multidisciplinary—see Appendix A and Hess (2018) for definitions.

[4] There was international variation within the interviewee data with VR5, VR6 and VR7 (all Vice Rectors of Research in universities elsewhere in Europe) highlighting difficulties within their own national funding bodies in funding interdisciplinary research and teaching.

[5] As women were in the minority in my leadership sample, I have chosen to identify all of my leadership respondents with female pronouns in order to preserve anonymity.

everything has to be interdisciplinary" (Quentin). But the experiences of other awardholders and the opinions expressed by Vice Rectors would contest this taken-for-grantedness. A notable counterpoint to those who regarded interdisciplinarity as mainstream was offered by Gina who saw herself and other individual interdisciplinarians like her as "a dying breed".

The "rhetoric" of interdisciplinarity and its decoupling from institutional practice was emphasised by awardholders who felt there was "some way to go" before researchers who took an interdisciplinary route no longer felt like they were taking risks with their career security and progression. Such observations from interviewees then led to discussions about how awardholders experienced their current university's attitudes towards interdisciplinarity. Despite our previous findings regarding the prevalence of the term within universities' policy documents (Bandola and Lyall 2015), some interviewees were quite unaware of institutional strategy, and this was not solely limited to the more junior members of staff. They were, however, sensitive to the dominant research policy narrative (see Chap. 1) that links interdisciplinarity with innovation:

> [I]t's something that's seen as a good thing isn't it, that it's creative and all that kind of stuff, but whether it actually happens. I feel that there are things that are trying to promote working across different departments but I would say they tend to be about trying to get us to work with technology, basically something that can produce intellectual property that they can then spin-off and get some money from. (Belinda)

Diana's department had initially regarded her as "a nuisance" and she had felt obliged to conform to the departmental norms but "changing tides" in terms of research funding opportunities and "what's popular" meant that she had once again been able to incorporate more social science into her research. When I probed Diana on what changes she had witnessed in attitudes towards interdisciplinary research, the dualism she depicted highlighted once again the misalignments in attitudes towards interdisciplinarity:

> [I]t's become both something that people view as having intrinsic value, and also it's become something you can exploit ... to get funding ... It feels at the moment like it's something that people are really being pushed to do, and how well we do it still I don't know. Sometimes it still feels a bit box-ticky, other times it feels like you're genuinely making some progress. (Diana)

An asymmetry in resources for supposedly interdisciplinary research endures. While Tristan pointed to increased funding, he also noted the unequal power dynamics, often linked to models of economic development, with the social sciences still not in the driving seat in interdisciplinary collaborations led by the natural sciences, and characterised by Julia as the humanities and social sciences "piggy-backing off the sciences" in order to access funds.

These conversations about how their university treated interdisciplinarity highlighted institutional differences between rhetoric and practice not just between different types of university but even within individual universities: both Tristan and Vera, who were from a non-Russell group university that had strong interdisciplinary roots, felt that interdisciplinary research was highly regarded while Selina and Una, from the same university but a different school, were much less positive about the putative interdisciplinary ethos of their particular research environment.

Departmental culture therefore matters. Interviewees who were based in geography departments talked about the inherently interdisciplinary nature of that discipline (Skole 2004), similarly anthropology and psychology. One could argue that all three are "portmanteau disciplines" that encompass both physical and social elements and interviewees based in these fields reported fewer problems with their interdisciplinary research and teaching. Problems arose when colleagues were trying to work across two paradigmatically different disciplinary departments and it is often such cultural barriers that are the hardest to overcome (Buanes and Jentoft 2009):

> Even things like the kind of way hierarchies operate are very different in the two departments that I'm in. In the medical school it's very top down, we're told this is the way it is and you have to sign-off grants through this person and do it in this way. As you would expect in the sociology school ... it's like "People's Republic of"... So everything is debated. (Julia)

So what I was hearing from these informants was that there was a lot of talk—and funding—around interdisciplinary research but not a lot of awareness on the part of institutions of how to really make it work. I was left with a strong sense of interdisciplinarians struggling to succeed in their careers with universities often relying on the good will of their staff in order to "muddle through".

Institutional Support Mechanisms

When I asked about the ways in which universities supported interdisciplinarity I heard about the roles of research offices, grant review panels and cross-university themes and institutes. I was told about support for networking events, "sandpits" and the availability of seedcorn funding to kick-start collaborations. Every one of the university research leaders (VR1-7, SR2) told me about the availability of internal funding; sometimes relatively small amounts to facilitate research networks across disciplines, sometimes sums sufficient to establish cross-faculty research institutes. Less frequently, I heard about strategic appointments (tenure track positions with a focus on cross-university working) or funding for interdisciplinary PhD studentships.

Undoubtedly, these research-intensive universities know how to catalyse large collaborative grant applications and have been successful in accessing the external public funding available to support interdisciplinary research, in the UK at least. What struck me was that these forms of institutional support were all essentially focusing on the input element. These were all about the loud, strategic voices encouraging people to respond to grant calls and this is developed further in Chap. 5 when I discuss the vagaries of "top down" initiatives.

Despite publicly advocating interdisciplinary strategies for research (and, increasingly, teaching—see Lyall et al. 2015), universities were portrayed as unwilling or unable to address the many administrative issues that impede interdisciplinarians in their daily work. These included (but were not limited to) supervision of graduate students who spanned two disciplines or departments leading to uncertainties regarding assessment procedures; the frustration of teaching across different schools; or accessing interdisciplinary studentships administered in other schools. Such aspects point to barriers to training the next generation of interdisciplinarians, which suggests universities did not learn sufficiently from the experience of the original joint studentships despite aspirations for changes to the training landscape (Meagher and Lyall 2005). What was missing from all of these conversations was any mention of the "softer side" of institutional support such as staff mentoring and career development so, in a chapter that is about the role of institutions in shaping interdisciplinary careers, only one element of potential support, in the form of research—rather than *researcher*—development was being reported.

RECOGNITION AND REWARD

Our conversations therefore moved on to what informants saw as barriers to interdisciplinarity or obstacles to interdisciplinary careers and this was a question asked to all interviewees across both samples. In a sense, their responses were myriad and the issues they raised already so well documented (e.g. Bruce et al. 2004; National Academy of Sciences 2005; Blackmore and Kandiko 2011; Benson et al. 2016) that one might question whether it is necessary to catalogue them again here. But, at the same time, I want to do justice to my interviewees' often heart-felt concerns, even if this means revisiting some already well-rehearsed topics.

Concerns about how interdisciplinary research is quantified under assessment schemes are pervasive (e.g. Kandiko and Blackmore 2008). For British interdisciplinarians their great nemesis remains "the REF". Taking place on a roughly six-yearly cycle, the Research Excellence Framework (REF)[6] is a national assessment of research quality across all UK universities. Structured around a series of peer review panels (termed "Units of Assessment"), this mechanism (and its precursor the Research Assessment Exercise, RAE) has always presented those whose work does not fall neatly within a single discipline domain with problems (Tait 1999). Despite planned changes for the next assessment in 2021,[7] "the REF" is ingrained in the minds of UK-based interdisciplinary researchers as a significant barrier to their career development. Awardholders expressed considerable uncertainty about the evaluation process, notably "where they will be returned", that is, which unit of assessment would consider their outputs, and spoke about the impact that this had on their academic progress and promotion, as illustrated by the examples below.

One of the technicalities of the REF process, and an aspect that has been somewhat open to interpretation by universities in the past, is the question of who should be deemed "REF-able". This hinges on how

---

[6] www.ref.ac.uk (accessed 19/12/18).

[7] Following the last evaluation exercise in 2014, the lead agency, the then Higher Education Funding Council for England (HEFCE) (now Research England), conducted a series of process reviews into the treatment of interdisciplinary research outputs (e.g. Adams et al. 2007) and established an Interdisciplinary Research Advisory Panel with a remit to "advise the REF team, REF panel chairs and the UK funding bodies on the approach to support the submission and assessment of interdisciplinary research in the REF". See https://www.ref.ac.uk/news/2017/interdisciplinaryresearchadvisorypanelannounced.html (accessed 8/1/19).

"independent" the researcher is considered to be but this varies between disciplines: in the social sciences, arts and humanities, research fellows often hold their own (albeit smaller) awards and pursue their own research interests whereas, in the natural and medical sciences, such junior staff are much more likely to be part of a team of researchers led by a Principal Investigator who holds the grant and sets the research agenda. One can envisage that research staff who span these different disciplinary traditions could be especially discomfited by this eligibility issue. This creates particular disquiet among staff on fixed-term contracts with, for example, Mariana, Selina and Una not feeling valued by their university because their contract status excluded them from the REF, despite all being successful and experienced researchers. Norman, Owen, Quentin and Tristan were generally less concerned by the REF process as their Unit of Assessment, in the past at least, had been judged sufficiently all-encompassing to provide a "safe space" in Quentin's words for interdisciplinary geographers. Even so, interdisciplinarians who could submit to other broad spectrum Units of Assessment cited specific examples of papers being excluded because they were considered "too interdisciplinary" and, as we see below, exclusion from the REF can result in significant career consequences.

These types of concerns were raised by the soft voices at various points in our conversations, not only in conjunction with the REF but related to peer review and publishing more generally. Interdisciplinary research is seen as a "high-risk, high-reward endeavor" (Leahey 2016) where scholars may achieve greater visibility (through citations of their publications) but are seen as less productive overall (Leahey et al. 2017). Even this issue of greater visibility may be open to question, as Yegros-Yegros et al. (2015) suggest that fellow academics may be reluctant to cite papers that are "heterodox", that is, too interdisciplinary, thus giving less credit to publications that may be seen as "too ground-breaking or challenging". Norman pinpointed another recognition concern when he remarked that he had never been invited to deliver keynote lectures because he did not belong to a particular sub-discipline that regarded him as the most relevant figure to give talks; an esteem issue that was neatly encapsulated as:

[Y]ou end up having a small name across a number of different areas rather than a big name in one area. (Iona)

University leaders (e.g. VR2) acknowledged that recognition was more difficult for interdisciplinarians: VR4 had a nuanced understanding of one of the key challenges of interdisciplinary peer review when tools or methods are taken from one discipline and applied in a different context which can provide new insights but may not be viewed as "cutting edge" and therefore fail to gain funding. This was recognised as an international problem (see also Lyall and King 2013), with VR5, for example, citing deficiencies in her national research funder in evaluating interdisciplinary research proposals and at the EU level where, in her experience as an evaluator, interdisciplinarity was treated "more like a fig leaf". This was confirmed by Reuben's astonishing encounter:

> [The] European Research Council ... pays lip service to interdisciplinarity but then forces you to nominate assessment panels ... So I ended up going through a biology panel ... one of the questions I got from one of the panel members was—"are you one of us"? And literally not words different to that. It was—"are you one of us"? ... it was a strange question to be asked like that but I somehow managed to muddle through. (Reuben)

The issue of inappropriate peer review goes beyond simply strange interview questions and can have real career consequences. Gina spoke at some length about being excluded from the last REF when one of her publications was graded poorly in her university's internal process, despite her co-author (from a different university) having the same paper highly rated. As a consequence, she was advised not to apply for promotion and steered way from publishing in sociology journals.[8] Gina's observations about the biases of the person in charge of review processes and the influence they have over whether one flourishes or not as an interdisciplinary scientist are hugely significant. Awardholders who were straddling medical and social science traditions found the REF particularly problematic, not least due to the emphases that the different disciplinary traditions place on the value of particular publication formats. Pressures to publish in certain outlets with higher impact factors lead interdisciplinary researchers to compromise the types of research they publish (Carina), resulting in publications "talking to the wrong people" (Belinda) and personal anxiety:

> [T]he REF does worry me but what can you do, I'm interdisciplinary at heart and it's far too late to start changing, nor do I think that would be a good thing. (Iona)

---

[8] Although ironically, as we shall see later in this chapter, her university regards her as suitably qualified to teach sociology to its undergraduate students.

Disciplines themselves can be regarded as "institutions" in the sense that they establish conventions that govern the practice of research (Castán Broto et al. 2009; Buanes and Jentoft 2009). The difficulty of publishing interdisciplinary research foregrounds many conflicting disciplinary norms: sole versus multi-author publications, the value attributed to high-impact journal articles over monographs, author order in journal articles, the dominance of a natural science culture where achieving a paper in *Nature* remains the gold standard even within an ostensibly interdisciplinary department; and the frustration of valuing "theory for theory's sake" despite an apparent desire to support research that has implications and impact for "the real world".[9]

WE ARE WHAT WE TEACH?

While universities are "simultaneously guardians of tradition and spaces for experimentation" (Vienni Baptista et al. 2018), conventional discipline-based governance prevails. The majority of university governance structures have been developed over time primarily to administer teaching curricula; research administration procedures and structures have been superimposed more recently in response to interdisciplinarity and in a "haphazard" fashion (Boardman and Bozeman 2007). Institutional arrangements generate "transaction costs" (Sá 2008) for academic staff and I therefore asked awardholders about the types of university structures that they had worked in, for example, research centres or departments, and whether they felt that the type of institutional setting might have affected their career as an interdisciplinary researcher.

Given that teaching in a discipline may present a challenge to interdisciplinarians, I was trying to determine whether interdisciplinary academics gravitate towards research centres rather than schools or departments that might be more teaching focused. If that was the case, then the consequence of long-term employment on research-only contracts, often associated with research centres, might be detrimental to their careers because they would be less likely to secure permanent jobs given their lack of teaching experience. This deficiency arises partly from a lack of opportunities, due to the nature of their contracts, and partly because they do not

---

[9] For a much fuller account of the mixed messages that academics receive around the balance between research excellence and impact see Bandola-Gill (2019).

have the single discipline expertise to fit neatly into a conventional teaching niche.

The existing literature on the role of research centres (in general) and interdisciplinary research centres (in particular) in academic career development is ambiguous. They are either a "benign addition" to existing university governance structures that increase productivity in terms of grants and publications without draining resources from departments (Biancani et al. 2018). Or they give rise to "role strain" (Boardman and Bozeman 2007) and are a source of "considerable tension" (Blomqvist et al. 2016) and perceived competition (Sá 2008) with respect to recruitment and resources between centres and collaborating departments, representing as they do examples of matrix management that cut across classical, vertical university structures (Sá 2008). Moreover, centre affiliation may have different effects at different career stages with senior, tenured faculty members appearing to benefit greatly from affiliation with a research centre (Sabharwal and Hu 2013), in contrast to more junior academic staff for whom employment in research centres (rather than departments) unhelpfully extends the "apprentice phase" (Laudel 2017).

Positive attributes of the research centre environment were identified by a number of awardholders (see Table 3.1) but there were contrasts in whether this research concentration was enabling or constraining for one's personal research (Fiona vs Quentin). Moreover, Selina's imminent departure from academia highlighted the problem for long-term research staff when an externally grant-funded research centre reaches the end of its funding period. Lengthy research centre contracts were considered unhelpful to career progression on the basis that being "disconnected from the mother ship" limited your options (VR3), most especially because a long-term research centre association reduced exposure to teaching (SR2). On the plus side, as in Vera's situation, working in a large school with a number of associated research centres had enabled progression

Table 3.1 Perceived benefits of a research centre environment

Accruing publications for promotion to lecturer (Anna)
Having a light teaching load and being able to concentrate on research (Carina, Diana, Norman)
Not having to teach in a discipline (Mariana)
An intellectually stimulating environment (Norman, Reuben, Vera)
Additional infrastructure support (Quentin)

without moving university. This intra-institutional mobility could be beneficial for interdisciplinary researchers and especially for those with caring responsibilities who may feel less able to move institution in order to advance their career although universities often value appointments from outside their ranks more than home-grown talent.

Conversations around the governance of teaching and the role this played in interdisciplinary careers revealed the extent to which our identities as academics are linked to what we teach, thus exposing a quandary for staff, especially in the research-intensive universities:

> Attitudes are changing but certainly when I was finishing my PhD the attitude was, do as little teaching as you can, focus on your research paper, people are only going to want to know about your grants and papers, they won't care if you've taught for ten years. (Carina)

When asked what she might have done differently, Carina would not have accepted a lectureship when she did. This contrasts with the expectation that most see a permanent position as a career asset although Katya, Julia and Una emphatically wanted research-only careers despite the fact that teaching remains the only secure route into a "permanent" academic contract in British universities. The irony of academics completing a research-based training in the form of a PhD and then being expected to teach—"which is a completely different skillset"—was not lost on Julia. Teaching may be seen as an important aspect of socialisation, contributing to an individual's sense of belonging to a group or department[10] but I heard from awardholders who felt wholly unqualified to teach:

> I immediately had to identify with a particular teaching team and research group, and that was sociology. I have never studied sociology in my life and so suddenly I was thrust in to having to teach undergraduates about quite in-depth sociology … the view of the management of the school is that if you're teaching at undergraduate level anyone can teach this subject. I don't agree with that because I think the students need more than somebody who is just regurgitating a book. (Gina)

Teaching outside of one's comfort zone/area of expertise places stress on interdisciplinary academics and this teaching imperative limits career

---

[10] Reinforcing Reuben's point of being seen as "one of us" but at a local, departmental level.

choices. While admitting that she probably could do it, Louisa was grateful that she had avoided being asked to teach the foundational theories of the discipline in which she was located as the prospect made her feel "insecure".

Vera identified the potential for strong links between interdisciplinary research and teaching, a theme that was generally absent from interviews with research leaders. But teaching across faculties was "pretty much impossible" for Quentin (despite being based in a university that has had a highly publicised interdisciplinary teaching strategy) while further institutional decoupling between rhetoric and practice in relation to the introduction of new interdisciplinary teaching was observed ("there's a lot of hassle from an admin logistics point of view, it's not exactly easy", Louisa). There were calls for universities to be more open to teaching different types of skills, a theme that I return to in Chap. 6 when I reflect on what we recognise as academic excellence.

Others had tried to keep their cross-institution teaching under the radar in order to build a promotion case ("I didn't really ask whether I could continue, I just carried on doing it", Anna) but this could cause issues with line management ("I should have got my line manager's approval for that, and she probably would have said 'no' because there's no benefit", Belinda). What is significant here for career prospects is the potential detriment to academic careers if early career researchers are prevented from developing their teaching practice. One could well argue that this is important for all researchers but especially so for young interdisciplinarians who may face an even more perilous career trajectory.

This reveals broader contractual issues within academia and indeed highlights variation among European universities.[11] Awardholder interviews reinforced the precarity of UK research contracts. While none of the issues summarised in Table 3.2 are necessarily unique to an interdisciplinary career, if the current governance structures of universities mean that interdisciplinary academics are more likely to spend longer in research-only contracts because of their lack of a clear teaching track, then they do indeed risk greater career disadvantage.

---

[11] Interviews with (non UK-based) LERU members confirmed that other EU universities place strict limits on how long postdocs can work in fixed-term contracts unlike my own experience (similar to that of several others in my interview sample) where the UK system does allow for research-only staff to be kept on notionally "open" contracts but only for the duration of external grant funding.

Table 3.2   Career consequences of short-term contracts

The constant cycling of research fellows though projects (Katya)
Limited development opportunities for research fellows (Fiona)
Salary restrictions
Reaching the top of your pay band (Una)
Becoming "too expensive to employ" (Erica)
Change in contractual status leading to cut in salary (Julia)
Lack of status associated with the research-only career track
Staff prevented from becoming PIs or PhD supervisors (Una)
Fewer opportunities to take on new areas of management responsibility (Mariana)

ROLES *AND* RESPONSIBILITIES

Assessment in its various forms is a thread that runs through any discussion of the role that institutions (see Footnote 1) play in interdisciplinary careers. While funding agencies are assuredly aware of the need to improve interdisciplinary evaluation processes (e.g. Lyall and King 2013), there is more that could be done to address this through improved interdisciplinary research management and leadership. This includes greater provision for capacity building and the facilitation of organisational learning (see Lyall et al. 2013). While research funders have important roles in ensuring the fairness of interdisciplinary review processes, they also have responsibilities towards those whom they fund. This demands greater awareness of the career implications of their funding instruments and a commitment to interdisciplinary funding throughout the academic life course. Yet, when I asked a representative of the main UK government research funding agencies how the newly formed UKRI planned to handle interdisciplinary peer review in the future she prevaricated, saying "it's such a complex area". When I asked to what extent developing capacity within our research community—to both undertake and lead—interdisciplinary research was part of a funder's remit, there was recognition of the potential "unintended consequences" of such funding instruments but a deflection back to university leadership:

> [R]ealistically, as a funder, you can only do so much … You can put the processes and the money … in place but, actually, the institution itself has to take responsibility. (SR3)

I found many of these conversations frustrating especially when VR6, for example, complained that the pace of change in interdisciplinary peer review was too slow. Senior research leaders, based in research-intensive universities and in senior positions within funding agencies, are surely the people best positioned to effect institutional change. This then epitomises one of the key misalignments within the system—or the "paradox of interdisciplinarity" (Woelert and Millar 2013; Weingart 2000) cited in Chap. 1—where interviewees juxtaposed incentives presented by the current interdisciplinary funding drivers in the UK with the hindrances of career recognition, reward and evaluation. My discussions with awardholders threw into sharp relief the many inconsistencies of current academic governance systems where academic identity and job security are largely linked to teaching but peer recognition is more usually connected to research. This dichotomy can have career-defining implications for individuals in situations where the contributions of interdisciplinary and single discipline research are weighted differently. So we train people to be interdisciplinary through their PhD but then restrict their career options because they do not have disciplinary expertise. The conclusion I draw from this is that we appear to be encouraging early career researchers to become interdisciplinary and then asking them to conform to what Anna termed "a more straightforward academic role". This seems entirely counterproductive, taking experts away from what they are good at:

> [T]hat's a big stress making somebody not from a particular discipline suddenly teach as if they were from that discipline … and it's also taking time away from being interdisciplinary and the values and the things that you can contribute through that. (Gina)

We observed this in our evaluations of these original studentship schemes and the current data indicate that the situation has not changed greatly in the past 10–15 years. Universities still need to find better ways of "squaring the circle" of both incentivising and then rewarding interdisciplinarity. The consequent wasted investment, if people trained at public expense to become interdisciplinary experts then fail to thrive in our current system, or make career compromises forcing them back into disciplines, is non-trivial. I return to this issue of institutional commitment in Chap. 6.

Talking Points
Discussions with interviewees reveal disparities between the rhetoric of interdisciplinarity and its decoupling from institutional practice. This highlights the responsibilities that those who promote interdisciplinarity have towards those whose careers they are influencing.

This raises questions, in particular, about the role that teaching currently plays in securing university contracts. What kind of job security do interdisciplinary researchers have compared with that of disciplinary experts? If institutions (universities and research funding agencies) want to facilitate interdisciplinarity yet teaching is typically focused on disciplinary education, what are the implications for hiring requirements for interdisciplinary faculty? What could be done to mitigate any negative consequences?

REFERENCES

Abbott, A. 2001. *Chaos of Disciplines.* Chicago: University of Chicago Press.

Adams, J., L. Jackson, and S. Marshall. 2007. *Bibliometric Analysis of Interdisciplinary Research.* Report to the Higher Education Funding Council for England, Leeds.

Bandola, J., and C. Lyall. 2015. *Interdisciplinarity in the Strategic Documents of the Russell Group Universities.* University of Edinburgh. Report to Researcher Experience Committee.

Bandola-Gill, Justyna. 2019. Between Autonomy and Engagement. Interpreting and Practising Knowledge Exchange in UK Academia. PhD Thesis, University of Edinburgh.

Benson, M.H., C.D. Lippitt, R. Morrison, B. Cosens, J. Boll, B.C. Chaffin, A.K. Fremier, R. Heinse, D. Kauneckis, T.E. Link, C.E. Scruggs, M. Stone, and V. Valentin. 2016. Five Ways to Support Interdisciplinary Work Before Tenure. *Journal of Environmental Studies and Sciences* 6 (2): 260–267.

Biancani, Susan, Linus Dahlander, Daniel A. McFarland, and Sanne Smith. 2018. Superstars in the Making? The Broad Effects of Interdisciplinary Centers. *Research Policy* 47 (3): 543–557.

Blackmore, Paul, and Camille B. Kandiko. 2011. Interdisciplinarity Within an Academic Career. *Research in Post-Compulsory Education* 16 (1): 123–134.

Blomqvist, C., C. Agrell, and C. Sandahl. 2016. Leadership Challenges of Strategic Research Centres in Relation to Degree of Institutionalisation. *Journal of Higher Education Policy and Management* 38 (6): 649–663.

Boardman, Craig, and Barry Bozeman. 2007. Role Strain in University Research Centers. *The Journal of Higher Education* 78 (4): 430–463.

Bruce, A., C. Lyall, J. Tait, and R. Williams. 2004. Interdisciplinary Integration in the Fifth Framework Programme. *Futures* 36 (4): 457–470.

Bryne, Sarah. 2014. Interdisciplinary Research: Why It's Seen As a Risky Route. *Higher Education*, February 19. https://www.theguardian.com/higher-education-network/blog/2014/feb/19/interdisciplinary-research-universities-academic-careers. Accessed 24 January 2019.

Buanes, Arild, and Svein Jentoft. 2009. Building Bridges: Institutional Perspectives on Interdisciplinarity. *Futures* 41: 446–454.

Castán Broto, Vanesa, Maya Gislason, and Melf-Hinrich Ehlers. 2009. Practising Interdisciplinarity in the Interplay Between Disciplines: Experiences of Established Researchers. *Environmental Science & Policy* 12 (7): 922–933.

ESRC. n.d. Multidisciplinarity on ESRC Grants. *ESRC*. https://esrc.ukri.org/files/about-us/performance-information/multidisciplinarity-on-esrc-grants/. Accessed 24 January 2019.

Hess, Andi. 2018. Two Types of Interdisciplinary Scholarship. *Integration and Implementation Insights*, February 6. https://i2insights.org/2018/02/06/two-types-of-interdisciplinarity/#andi-hess. Accessed 24 January 2019.

Hulkes, A. 2018. The Arc of Funding. *ESRC*, June 26. https://blog.esrc.ac.uk/?s=the+arc+of+funding. Accessed 24 January 2019.

Kandiko, C.B., and P. Blackmore. 2008. Institutionalising Interdisciplinary Work in Australia and the UK. *Journal of Institutional Research* 14 (1): 87–95.

Laudel, G. 2017. How Do National Career Systems Promote or Hinder the Emergence of New Research Lines? *Minerva* 55 (3): 341–369.

Leahey, E. 2016. From Sole Investigator to Team Scientist: Trends in the Practice and Study of Research Collaboration. *Annual Review of Sociology* 42: 81–100.

Leahey, E., C.M. Beckman, and T.L. Stanko. 2017. Prominent but Less Productive: The Impact of Interdisciplinarity on Scientists' Research. *Administrative Science Quarterly* 62 (1): 105–139.

Lowe, Philip, and Jeremy Phillipson. 2006. Reflexive Interdisciplinary Research: The Making of a Research Programme on the Rural Economy and Land Use. *Journal of Agricultural Economics* 57 (2): 165–184.

Lyall, C., L. Meagher, J. Bandola, and A. Kettle. 2015. *Interdisciplinary Provision in Higher Education: Current and Future Challenges*. Report to Higher Education Academy.

Lyall, Catherine, and Emma King. 2013. *International Good Practice in the Peer Review of Interdisciplinary Research*. Report to the RCUK Research Directors Group.

Lyall, Catherine, Ann Bruce, Wendy Marsden, and Laura Meagher. 2013. The Role of Funding Agencies in Creating Interdisciplinary Knowledge. *Science and Public Policy* 40: 62–71.

Meagher, Laura, and Catherine Lyall. 2005. *Evaluation of the ESRC/NERC Interdisciplinary Research Studentship Scheme*. Report to ESRC.

National Academy of Sciences. 2005. *Facilitating Interdisciplinary Research*. Washington, DC: National Academies Press.

Sá, Creso M. 2008. 'Interdisciplinary Strategies' in U.S. Research Universities. *Higher Education* 55: 537–552.

Sabharwal, Meghna, and Qian Hu. 2013. Participation in University-Based Research Centers: Is It Helping or Hurting Researchers? *Research Policy* 42: 1301–1311.

Skole, David L. 2004. Geography As a Great Intellectual Melting Pot and the Preeminent Interdisciplinary Environmental Discipline. *Annals of the Association of American Geographers* 94 (4): 739–743.

Tait, J. 1999. Help for the Academic Nomads in Search of Their Own Sympathetic Tribe. *Times Higher Education*, March 5.

Vienni Baptista, Bianca, Federico Vasen, and Juan Carlos Villa Soto. 2018. Interdisciplinary Centers in Latin American Universities: The Challenges of Institutionalization. *Higher Education Policy*. https://doi.org/10.1057/s41307-018-0092-x.

Weingart, Peter. 2000. Interdisciplinarity: The Paradoxical Discourse. In *Practising Interdisciplinarity*, ed. Peter Weingart and Nico Stehr, 25–41. Toronto: University of Toronto Press.

Woelert, Peter, and Victoria Millar. 2013. The 'Paradox of Interdisciplinarity' in Australian Research Governance. *Higher Education* 66: 755–767.

Yegros-Yegros, A., I. Rafols, and P. D'Este. 2015. Does Interdisciplinary Research Lead to Higher Citation Impact? The Different Effect of Proximal and Distal Interdisciplinarity. *PLoS One* 10 (8): e0135095.

CHAPTER 4

The Nets We Weave: Consequences for Interdisciplinary Capacity Building

A QUESTION OF TIMING

One of the justifications for a qualitative research design is that it can prompt unanticipated outcomes. This was the case with my first interview with a Vice Rector of Research, as a result of which I subsequently asked all of my leadership interviewees the question *When is the right time in an academic career to become interdisciplinary?*

This proved to be one of the most illuminating aspects of my study, revealing contradictions not just between the "loud and soft voices" within my dataset but a crucial point of disagreement among university leadership.[1] As such, this question of timing opened up a core debate in the governance of interdisciplinary academic careers:

> I don't think interdisciplinarity is a good training base … If you don't get a deep disciplinary training, it's really difficult to know what you don't know … I love to have PhD students excited by the bigger questions and I'd love to involve them in a little snippet of it but they have to, if you like, do their journeyman-ship. (VR1)

---

[1] The Vice Rectors of Research and other senior research representatives, who were interviewed as part of this study, had been selected from among a group of 23 long established, European research-intensive universities who had quite recently been engaged in the production of a report on interdisciplinary research convened by their representative body (LERU 2016). This shared backdrop perhaps heightens the surprise at the quite polarised views expressed by these leadership interviewees on this question of timing.

The "sweet spot" (VR1) to become interdisciplinary was once the individual had made a distinctive, discipline-based, contribution to scholarship and was developing their own research agenda at the post-doctoral/early career lecturer stage.

This then begs the question of how do you know what your distinctive contributions to scholarship could be if you have only been trained to think in one way? Our discipline shapes the questions we ask: "What a discipline does not have concepts for; it is neither able to see nor inclined to look for … And what the discipline cannot see, it has no remedy for" (Buanes and Jentoft 2009). Or, put another way:

> The kinds of nets we know how to weave determine the kinds of nets we cast. These nets, in turn, determine the kinds of fish we catch. (Eisner 1982, p. 49)[2]

Other interviewees partly went on to address this conundrum but, as I discuss below, their responses were ambiguous.

What VR1 is advocating is that, at some point in their 30s, someone who has been trained as a discipline expert suddenly acquires the skills to become interdisciplinary especially when many of these skills (see e.g. Bennett et al. 2018) are tacit. Yet is it reasonable to expect someone trained as a specialist in a very narrow field to "know what they don't know" if they have not had their minds opened up to different ways of thinking and the possibilities presented by different disciplinary paradigms?

I will come back to this next point but it is worth making it now: none of the 22 interdisciplinary studentship awardholders whom I interviewed for this book looked back over their careers and said that they wished they had not followed an interdisciplinary route from the outset, nor did they discourage others from following in their footsteps, contrary to the "feelings of dismay and regret" that McBee and Leahey (2017) suggest they might experience.

VR2 talked about "this academic craze for interdisciplinarity" and how it was driven by funding, without any concern for career destinations. But an interdisciplinary career was not always seen as a disadvantage and other Vice Rectors were open to developing an interdisciplinary approach at any

---

[2] I am grateful to Myra Strober (Strober 2011) for this quotation.

stage in an academic career, precisely countering VR1's putative transition point[3]:

> I've always observed it as not really a conscious choice that—you know, today I'm a disciplinary scientist and then I'm going to wake up tomorrow because I've hit 30, because I've been promoted to be a senior lecturer or whatever ... And now magically I'm a multidisciplinary [sic] researcher. (VR3)

Starting interdisciplinarity early was not necessarily seen as detrimental to one's career or to research quality although this was not unanimous: while VR7 acknowledged that colleagues did not all share her opinion she, herself, was adamant that we are losing potential in our education and in our research if we do not allow for the possibility of different types of academic careers.

Other respondents were self-contradictory, initially suggesting that interdisciplinarity could happen at any stage in an academic career but then qualifying this with the following orchestral analogy:

> First of all, any individual player is absolutely world leading in the mastery of their own instrument and they've only done that through long hours of engagement with that instrument and practice. Second, they have to be cognisant that they are part of a larger group and the purpose of the larger group is more than them as soloists but as an entity that is producing something together. And part of that then is the third piece, which is the sensitivity and sensibility that, at all stages in what they're doing, they recognise that their training, their expertise is in service to that larger goal, so that they are cognisant that there is more to the world than their own actual discipline. (VR4)

So, what I take from this is that the time to become interdisciplinary was once the individual had "mastered their instrument", that is, developed discipline-based excellence. According to this stance, it is the post-doctoral stage that should open up interdisciplinary opportunities, starting from firm discipline-based foundations but with a caveat that the notion of interdisciplinarity should have been introduced during the earlier phases of educational training. This should not be optional and students should

---

[3] I did, however, feel that VR3 was primarily talking about her own field which was perhaps more inherently interdisciplinary than some of the less proximate combinations of discipline described in Chap. 1.

be "exposed to courses" outside of their main discipline from the undergraduate level (VR6).

This account represents interdisciplinary research as teams of discipline experts working together and this was justified by VR6 on the grounds of graduate employability, at least within academic contexts. Interdisciplinary PhD training was considered acceptable for those who were going to work outside of academia (SR2), which raises the question of what careers we are training PhD students for. The suggestion that we are only training PhD students to follow the traditional path into academia (as implied by VR1 and VR6) no longer holds true. Acknowledging that the majority of their PhD graduates found work outside of academia, SR2 conceded that it might be "really good for them to work more interdisciplinarily" but for the "1% who stay in academia, it's perhaps not so" (SR2).

However, given what we learned in Chap. 2 about awardholders' apparent lack of career planning, this could be problematic, requiring PhD students to know from the outset of their studies whether they would want to pursue an academic career or not. By this account, these interdisciplinary graduates are "really good" and "prepared very well to work somewhere" (SR2)—just not in academia. How might we expect to staff interdisciplinary research centres (of the type SR2's university was actively funding), if we do not train PhD students to be interdisciplinary. If these research centres only employ young researchers who have been trained in a very narrow way does it follow that research group leaders then have to re-educate them in order to contribute to the interdisciplinary groups? This is certainly the position of Colin Campbell, Director of the James Hutton Institute, who has been quoted as saying: "We are very often starting from scratch with disciplinary-trained scientists and trying to convert them into interdisciplinary scientists" (Palmer 2018).

To varying degrees, the focus for Vice Rectors (VR1, VR2, VR5 and VR6) was on disciplinary excellence but with early sensitisation to interdisciplinary research. This "sensitisation" might be seen as an appreciation of how other disciplines worked: VR2 made sure that her own research fellows spent time in collaborators' labs but this occurred at the post-doctoral level and her examples were very focused on her own laboratory-based experience. For someone who was Vice Rector of Research for a full spectrum university, VR2 was not alone in seemingly having an outlook and frame of reference that was quite discipline specific.

Ongoing "siloed thinking" was cited as the main obstacle to interdisciplinary research but the connection between this and the belief that interdisciplinarity should only be fully embraced after the PhD went unacknowledged. I return to this question of whether exposure to interdisciplinarity "by courses", as promoted by VR6, is adequate preparation for an interdisciplinary career in the final section of this chapter.

Finally, among this interview group, I interviewed someone who held a senior position within one of the UK research funders that promotes interdisciplinary research but does not appear to reflect greatly on the impact that this might have on academic careers. She recognised that differences in opinion over when to become interdisciplinary would lead to tensions in situations where the visions of university research leaders were decoupled from the many funding schemes that encourage researchers to work in an interdisciplinary way. She further acknowledged that our institutions do not do enough to facilitate interdisciplinarity. Nevertheless, I did not gain the impression that this funder felt that it was their role to change this situation, highlighting yet again the misalignment between intent and actual practice in the governance of interdisciplinarity.

Given this further apparent decoupling of policy and practice, VR2 was right to say that, in the UK at least, funders are not thinking about the impact this type of interdisciplinary research training can have on the trainee but we also need to consider that universities may need to change their understandings of what an academic career looks like—that excellence is no longer solely about having detailed, expert knowledge in a narrow area. What the twenty-first century demands is academics who can communicate, apply knowledge, understand how different forms of knowledge contribute and have an understanding of how to bring all that together. So it is not a case of having "a bit of this and a bit of this and a bit of this" (VR2) but teaching young scholars to build synergies between different forms of knowledge.

GOOD CAREER PREPARATION?

So what did the awardholders think about this question of when to become an interdisciplinary researcher?[4] Only one of the awardholder interviewees echoed Vice Rectors' desire for discipline specialists able to work in interdisciplinary teams:

---

[4] I had not explicitly asked this in the first phase of my interviews but I did ask two questions about experiences of their doctoral training: *How effective was your PhD training as preparation for your subsequent (interdisciplinary) career?* Then towards the end of the

[W]hat people want isn't interdisciplinary people. What they want is disciplinary people with a strong background in a discipline who can work in an interdisciplinary environment or an interdisciplinary team. (Mariana)

The specific question of whether their interdisciplinary graduate studies had been an effective grounding for their academic careers attracted positive responses, for example:

- it had opened up job opportunities (Belinda)
- it was a good "platform" for current research which was a continuation of PhD topic (Erica, Iona)
- it had been "hugely effective" (Diana)
- it had enabled researchers to understand perspectives beyond a narrow discipline domain (Louisa, Katya)

The question of whether they would recommend this type of PhD training to others received either a resounding "yes" from awardholders or positive responses with modest provisos, for example:

- making sure the supervision is appropriate and that the PhD is truly interdisciplinary and not just "tokenistic" (Belinda, Diana, Mariana, Norman, Reuben)
- being aware of the potential additional challenges (Norman, Owen)
- if they want a research career (as opposed to one that involves teaching) (Gina)
- if the research topic requires it (Katya, Tristan)
- it depends on the individual (Julia)

There was enthusiasm for this form of PhD as effective training for an academic career from awardholders who spoke about the importance of the broader learning environment:

[I]t's not necessarily the formal training process but it's the kind of informal culture and environment and the people you interact with regularly. (Norman)

interview I asked: *Would you recommend a similar style of PhD to others a preparation for an academic career?* In some cases, I rephrased the question, asking: *Has that type of PhD training been good preparation for the type of job that you find yourself doing now?* I have therefore used these questions as proxies for the timing question so that what the awardholders said on this topic was spontaneously generated rather than in response to a specific question.

Such responses refute those Vice Rectors who think it is possible to "become" interdisciplinary later in your career by emphasising that PhD training is an apprenticeship into a discipline and the culture of that discipline as discussed further in the final section when I pick up this theme of "socialisation" (Felt et al. 2012).

In Retrospect

One of my final questions during the awardholder interviews was: *What would you do differently looking back at your career so far?*

While some of the responses were quite unequivocal with interviewees professing themselves to be happy with where they found themselves in their careers, others were tempered by hindsight. Diana was in a good place when I interviewed her, having recently secured a large interdisciplinary fellowship but acknowledged that it had taken her time to reach this stance.

Significantly, when asked this question, none of my awardholders said that they regretted their choice of PhD studentship or the interdisciplinary direction that their career had taken. They did talk about how they might have finessed their career development and offered lessons based on that experience. So, when awardholders reasoned how they might have acted differently in retrospect, I heard examples of issues related to poor hiring decisions when new PIs were recruiting research staff for the first time and concerns about the impact of maternity leave and family responsibilities on careers, neither of which would be unique to an interdisciplinary career. What many of these responses were highlighting were not regrets about their career path but deficits in the ways that their institutions supported academic careers as I explain in Chap. 6. So, rather than misgivings about following the interdisciplinary route, I heard about the desire to have had more self-confidence in taking that path and how this linked to one's sense of identity (see Chap. 2):

> [M]aybe I should have not been so hung up about not being a proper anthropologist, but just kind of gone for it and been a bit more confident about it and maybe published—I've never published in any actual anthropology journals, for example, because I always thought I'm not good enough for that. (Louisa)

A lot of Gina's anxiety stemmed from the teaching requirements placed on her by her university and the mismatch between that teaching and her interdisciplinary expertise (see Chap. 3), and, in retrospect, she said she might have preferred to steer her career more towards the research-focused institutions. For Belinda, it was about the nature of her role as a qualitative researcher working in a medical setting, which meant that she did not produce as many publications as her peers. In retrospect, Belinda felt that she would have advanced further in her career if she had not taken her current post. Reuben was really very sanguine in his response:

> Ah, many, many things (LAUGHS). But also in a way nothing … with hindsight you kind of think, I shouldn't have worried about that so much. (Reuben)

While judged beneficial, interdisciplinary training was made harder for those who found that they were not a good "fit" with either supervisors or host departments (e.g. Mariana, Diana). This points to a governance issue and highlights the learning that universities need to embrace if they are going to train interdisciplinary researchers effectively and really "walk the talk", a point to which we return in Chap. 6 when I introduce the interdisciplinary logic of commitment.

This question did provide an important counterpoint to earlier conversations about whether awardholders had developed a strategic approach to their careers (see Chap. 2). A common thread running through responses was the admission that, in retrospect, respondents wished they had been more strategic or selective:

> I'd have said "no" to a few more things when I started my lectureship … it's inevitable when you're new, you want to say "yes" and get involved in things and, as an interdisciplinary researcher, I think it's important that you have to say "yes" because if there's a new collaboration, you don't know what's going to come out of it, whether it's going to be a success or not. But I think I could have been a bit more strategic about what I said "yes" to initially. (Owen)

When I probed Vera on this by asking if she felt she would have reached senior lecturer more quickly if she had been more "conformist", her response was that some of her interdisciplinary "inclinations" had held her back from greater recognition of her work and that a more traditional academic career path would have opened up avenues for progressing further more easily. Vera was such a passionate advocate for interdisciplinarity and had talked earlier in the interview about always having been interdisciplinary, even from schooldays, that I cannot imagine that what she is saying here is that she would not have followed those "interdisciplinary inclinations" but that she would have presented them differently in order to "conform" to the dominant academic norms.

While selectivity certainly might be more of a problem for interdisciplinary researchers, it is by no means unique to that group and many academics have a problem saying "no" in my experience. What I was hearing was a need for more institutional support and training for career building and this, again, is not unique to interdisciplinarity.

The above responses, and others like them (e.g. Una who spoke about wishing she had started to bid for grants earlier in her career; or Katya who would have benefited from some guidance on the culture of working in medical research) indicate a desire to be a smarter, more strategic interdisciplinary academic rather than regrets about following an interdisciplinary route, per se, and speak to the need for better mentoring, management and guidance of young interdisciplinary researchers who are starting out on their careers rather than urging them to delay that step. The themes of mentoring and role models resurface in Chap. 6.

Finding a Niche

This chapter has revealed a fundamental misalignment between some research leaders and the awardholders on the question of when an academic career should "become interdisciplinary". On the one hand, there is the view that this is something that should be delayed until careers are firmly established. On the other hand, when asked to look back over their careers, not one of the awardholders whom I interviewed said that they regretted taking that early step into interdisciplinarity. But one issue raised by awardholder interviews that resonates with some of the Vice Rectors is a concern about where these researchers "belong". When Gina talked about finding her identity in Chap. 2, she highlighted the discomfort that others feel when interdisciplinarians do not conform to disciplinary standards. But when Julia, Quentin and others talk about this issue of finding a niche it is clear that some people do not want to be "pigeon-holed". Not "fitting" can be an intellectual advantage, enabling greater critical capabilities to flourish, and although awardholders appreciated the benefits of specialisation and admired researchers who had carved out their own niche, they also realised that it did not suit their temperament and were "interested in too many things". However, even those very committed to interdisciplinarity had encountered colleagues who decried their ability to "make a name" for themselves as academics and admitted that "being jack-of-all-trades and master of none might not be in your favour" (Vera).

Mariana's advice to others was probably the most closely aligned with the concerns of some of the Vice Rectors:

> [D]on't jump around too much or, if you do, be aware that will make your life more difficult, maybe try and build a bit more of a track record, a bit of a niche, so people know why they'd go to you specifically, what you can bring to research. (Mariana)

So, although none of the awardholder interviewees explicitly supported the idea that the turn to interdisciplinarity should be delayed in one's career, these concerns about finding one's niche do highlight the discomfort of not complying with current academic career norms.

At the heart of many of the Vice Rectors' concerns lies a tension between breadth and depth of knowledge, leading to the view that, in order to be academically "excellent", one must have an in-depth knowledge of a single discipline. The corollary is then that interdisciplinarians must have a shallower expertise as epitomised by VR2's earlier comment about them only knowing multiple different "bits" or the commonplace trope of interdisciplinarians being "jacks of all trades". This risks interdisciplinary work being seen as a "sideline" (Fischer et al. 2012) or "the dabbling of a dilettante" (Lattuca 2002) rather than serious scholarship.

Such scepticism overlooks the fact that at the crux of good interdisciplinary research lies not a shallow knowledge of myriad topics but a detailed understanding of how to make different forms of knowledge work together synergistically (especially in the case of transdisciplinary research, the inclusion of lay or practitioner knowledge). This highlights a fundamental misunderstanding of the roles played by interdisciplinary researchers who are specialists in their own right and not simply academic "generalists". Yet the "the canonical narrative" of the single discipline expert prevails (Cuevas-Garcia 2016, p. 188).

The rather disparaging phrase "jack of all trades, master of none", which tripped off the lips of even my committed interdisciplinarians, is one that is over used—and indeed misused—in the context of interdisciplinarity (e.g. Cuevas-Garcia 2015, 2016; Lau and Pasquini 2008) where the unique strength of interdisciplinarians is not their knowledge of several disciplines but their more tacit, integrative skills and panoptic perspectives.

Interdisciplinary expertise goes beyond the type of "T-shaped" individuals (van der Zwaan 2017, p. 156)[5] that VR6 favoured in terms of a disciplinary core but reaching out to other disciplines. People, who have been recipients of the UK Research Councils' interdisciplinary studentships, and similar postgraduate training, should be regarded as catalysts, bridge builders and integrators who are good at bringing people together and making links. Interdisciplinarity also has the advantage of fostering diversity within academic communities: graduate students have a tendency to become "clones" of their mentor or supervisor (Blackburn et al. 1981). However, as Quentin, Norman and SR1 all observed, this is less likely to be the case when a researcher follows a more interdisciplinary route and this can yield a diversity dividend:

> [B]eing only in your discipline is also risky in terms of getting tenure … if you only reproduce what people tell you to do, you probably won't be so successful in terms of what you bring … there are some people willing to take more risk to really do things that are a bit unconventional. It's risky but, I mean, staying in the foot of your supervisor, doing what has been done is also risky. (SR1)

The notion of the "traditional" academic career is discussed further in Chap. 6 but before we leave this issue of timing we need to lay to rest some misconceptions about "becoming interdisciplinary".

KNOWLEDGE ACQUISITION VERSUS SOCIALISATION

When we evaluated the original studentship scheme, one supervisor described how

> [w]e cannot resolve any of the big challenges we face in the future with just people who have sat in silos coming together. We need young professionals who have come up in this way… to see the interconnections. (Meagher and Lyall 2009, p. 35)

---

[5] A T-shaped individual demonstrates a strong disciplinary training (the vertical part of the "T") and reaches out to form connections with other disciplines in order to develop joint solutions (the horizontal bar of the "T") in contrast to I-shaped individuals who exhibit only deep but narrow disciplinary expertise. This terminology is variously attributed but most likely originates from McKinsey and Company business consultants in the 1980s.

Awardholders were seen as being "broader thinkers, more innovative, and more open to different ideas or approaches" (Meagher and Lyall 2009, p. 35) in comparison with postgraduates funded through the Research Councils' open competitions.

This resonates with the reworking of the classical allegory[6] that divides scholars into two categories: "hedgehogs", who perceive the world through a single lens and "foxes", who draw on a wide variety of experiences (Berlin 1953). If, as Frodeman (2014) suggests, "Skill at interdisciplinary work ... becomes a matter of character rather than methodology", can this metaphor of hedgehogs and foxes be extended to assess how we, as a community, best develop the capacity to undertake such research, while recognising that disciplines will continue to exist?

There are significant differences of opinion over whether interdisciplinarity is an approach that can be taught from rubrics (e.g. Repko 2008; Bammer 2013) or whether success in interdisciplinarity must always demand a bespoke, more nuanced, approach. In order to build resilient research communities, do we need more "foxes"—researchers who range across many areas and traditions—or should academia continue to specialise in monodisciplinary "hedgehogs" who each focus on one substantive and theoretical domain? And the next question that we then need to answer, in order to address some of the Vice Rectors' concerns, is *when* should that development or transition take place?

Despite trends towards interdisciplinarity, the view persists that universities still prefer to employ discipline-based experts (Nelson 2011) and that young academics seeking to follow an interdisciplinary path risk losing job security (Rhoten and Parker 2004). Yet, more recently, it has been suggested that interdisciplinary dissertation research actually increases the individual's chance of obtaining an academic position (Millar 2013). This dichotomy is echoed especially by researchers working in climate change such as Benson et al. (2016) who encourage faculty to address interdisciplinary research problems early on and "[lay] the groundwork for a successful, long-term career in such endeavors". Hein et al. (2018) suggest that the number of young researchers now being trained in interdisciplinary science outstrips the ability of institutional governance structures to accommodate them, leading to both perceived and real impediments to interdisciplinary career paths. This question of timing reflects a live debate

---

[6]The fox knows many things, but the hedgehog knows one big thing (Archilochus, 700 BC).

within the UK academic establishment that suggests a fundamental misunderstanding about how interdisciplinarians—and indeed academic researchers in general—are "trained".

Interdisciplinary scholars debate the extent to which an individual can indeed "learn" to become interdisciplinary (Fam et al. 2017) and there is a widely held appreciation that this requires both the acquisition of an array of skills and certain personality traits that predispose the individual to interdisciplinary (or transdisciplinary) aptitudes (Augsburg 2014; Bruce et al. 2004). Fam et al. (2017) report how participants in their study overwhelmingly articulated the need to consider "more than skills" and referred to the "attitudes, orientations, temperaments, dispositions and predispositions" required to build interdisciplinary capacities.

These authors stress that such researchers do not "appear from heaven" but require skills development—often through "learning by doing"—and question the extent to which such skills and dispositions can indeed be "taught" (Fam et al. ibid.). Others portray research as a "craft" and liken the process of acquiring research skills to an "apprenticeship" (Castán Broto et al. 2009; see also Laudel and Gläser 2008). We thus need to think of doctoral programmes not just as "training" in a particular knowledge base but as a process of "socialisation" where students learn about the cultural norms, language and behaviours through both the taught curriculum and research opportunities and also engagement with other researchers (Holley 2015; Boden et al. 2011; Felt et al. 2012). Such conventions are not learned from reading textbooks (Castán Broto et al. 2009), leading Holley (2015) to advocate that "it would be a mistake to assume that interdisciplinary proficiency results from the accumulation of disciplinary knowledge".

Acquiring facility in another discipline is often equated to "learning another language" but such second language learners will never become truly fluent. It has further been suggested that placing too much emphasis on developing "a common language" in interdisciplinary collaborations may be misguided as it can lead to stagnation rather than innovation.[7] Hirsch Hadorn suggests that the focus should be on training people to become "multilingual" and, indeed, Louisa, who was bilingual, equated the intellectual stimulation of an interdisciplinary training to the benefits of bilingualism.

---

[7] Professor Gertrude Hirsch Hadorn, ETH Zurich speaking at ITD Conference Leuphana University Luneburg, September 2017.

The process of "becoming interdisciplinary" is not like the analogy of turning on a tap. As awardholders noted, learning to appreciate how other disciplines "think" so that we begin to understand their "habits of mind" (Strober 2011, p. 4) takes time, a theme to which we return in Chap. 5. This process of "enculturation" (Collins and Evans 2007, p. 24) is, these authors argue, "the only way to master an expertise which is deeply laden with tacit knowledge" as the rules will not necessarily be written down and can only be understood through practice.

Different disciplinary paradigms may appear incommensurable. Paterson had managed to span psychology, psychiatry and neurology in his PhD because those disciplines "speak very similar languages" but he had struggled to foster interdisciplinary collaborations with philosophers and sociologists. Julia attributed such difficulties to the "conventions" within each of the disciplines and the hazards of disciplinary practitioners "reifying" those conventions in ways that make it harder for those outside the discipline to collaborate.

If we then relate this to Collins and Evans' (ibid., p. 24) "interactional" and "contributory" expertise, we might consider that lifelong interdisciplinarians, such as my awardholder interviewees, demonstrate the ability to "contribute" to a knowledge domain by virtue of their training and socialisation (or enculturation) whereas discipline specialists are able only to "interact" with other disciplines as part of interdisciplinary collaborations.

Interdisciplinarity was talked about in interviews as something that was inherent or "embodied" which implies that there is, moreover, a distinctive contributory expertise in being interdisciplinary. As noted previously, the unique strength of interdisciplinarians is not their knowledge of several disciplines but their more tacit, integrative skills, sometimes termed "meta-skills" (Skills Development Scotland 2018):

> [W]e came to the conclusion that it was probably far easier to train and work as interdisciplinary scholars than it is often to bring together a team of people from a different discipline to try and get them to work across boundaries. ... you need people who can embody interdisciplinarity at some level, that have that kind of ability or confidence or willingness to go and read widely, research widely, think widely ... because it's not just about skills, because skills you can pick up as you go along ... there's definitely a mind set. (Norman)

This refutes the "disciplinary excellence with sensitisation" model where Vice Rectors seek to give an interdisciplinary orientation to discipline-grounded researchers (perhaps "through courses" as championed by VR6 earlier). Such an approach does not allow for a process of enculturation. The doctoral experience is not simply about learning skills and facts and becoming an expert in a particular topic or technique, it is also about shaping the type of scholar you will become: Katya made the trenchant observation that her interdisciplinary training had given her "the skills to not see the sociology in everything". Reflecting on the differences between knowledge and understanding, our understanding of a topic is based partly on "what else we already understand" (Collini 2012, p. 67). Thus, if one were to "become interdisciplinary" at a later career stage, it is not "sensitisation" that is required but "re-conditioning", as noted by Colin Campbell earlier.

In contrast, the "hybridisation" model, which seeks to enhance interdisciplinary capabilities by training early career researchers who are interdisciplinary from the outset—as my awardholder interviewees were—recognises that there are embodied dispositions and shared cultures—a "habitus" (Bourdieu 1990, p. 9) that shapes our actions as interdisciplinarians. This gives hybrid interdisciplinarians "a feel for the game" because they have already learned the "doxa"—the written and unwritten rules—(Bourdieu 2000, p. 15) in order to exist in that field and have the necessary "cognition without consciousness" (Bourdieu 1990, p. 12). Kuhn (1970, pp. 182–185) characterises this as a "matrix" that encompasses not just the "symbolic generalizations" shared by a scientific community but the communal values, beliefs and techniques.

As already observed, we often do not make the distinction between individual interdisciplinarity and collaborative interdisciplinarity[8] sufficiently explicit. Yet, as Hess (2018) notes (and Norman alluded to above), the resources and methods required to address these two categories of interdisciplinary work are quite different. In particular, they rest on quite different foundations and it is this that some Vice Rectors are failing to recognise when they suggest that interdisciplinary careers can be launched once the individual has achieved "disciplinary excellence".

What this chapter has shown is both a misalignment between the "loud and soft voices" on the optimal time to launch an interdisciplinary career and a lack of consensus on this topic among the leaders of some of Europe's most prestigious, research-intensive universities. How do these Vice Rectors expect to be able to turn hedgehogs into foxes mid-way through

---

[8] Hess (2018) terms this second category "interdisciplinary dialogue and team science".

an academic career? This represents a naïve understanding of interdisciplinarity and people's motivations and dispositions. It ignores the important socialisation aspects of the PhD apprenticeship, which is much more than just learning a discipline in order to become excellent in a narrow field. Significantly, this attitude could also have consequences for the progress of science since a key insight from Kuhn (1970, p. 90) is that it is the younger members of a scientific community who are more likely to abandon an old paradigm and adopt a new one:

> [I]t makes sense to get involved in interdisciplinary research sooner rather than later … it's about being exposed to different ideas and different approaches … the longer you go without experience of these things, they're more difficult. (Reuben)

Talking Points

When to develop interdisciplinary skills is a significant issue. University leaders disagree on this question of timing and this reveals some fundamental misunderstandings about the nature of interdisciplinary knowledge, how this is acquired, and the skills that interdisciplinary researchers offer.

What steps can institutions take in order to catalyse or support long-term interdisciplinary capacity building? Should this take place through formal degree training? Through short courses or other events focused on the processes of interdisciplinarity? How could skills of interdisciplinary researchers be developed—and valued—explicitly? What tactics and safety nets need to be deployed to ensure that this adds value to academic careers rather than making them vulnerable?

REFERENCES

Augsburg, Tanya. 2014. Becoming Transdisciplinary: The Emergence of the Transdisciplinary Individual. *World Futures* 70 (3–4): 233–247.
Bammer, Gabriele. 2013. *Disciplining Interdisciplinarity. Integration and Implementation Sciences for Researching Complex Real-World Problems.* Canberra: ANU E Press.
Bennett, L.M., H. Gadlin, and C. Marchand. 2018. *Collaboration and Team Science Field Guide.* 2nd ed. Bethesda: National Cancer Institute.

Benson, M.H., C.D. Lippitt, et al. 2016. Five Ways to Support Interdisciplinary Work Before Tenure. *Journal of Environmental Studies and Sciences* 6 (2): 260–267.

Berlin, Isaiah. 1953. *The Hedgehog and the Fox: An Essay on Tolstoy's View of History*. London: Weidenfeld & Nicolson.

Blackburn, Robert T., David W. Chapman, and Susan M. Cameron. 1981. "Cloning" in Academe: Mentorship and Academic Careers. *Research in Higher Education* 15 (4): 315–327.

Boden, D., M. Borrego, and L.K. Newswander. 2011. Student Socialization in Interdisciplinary Doctoral Education. *Higher Education* 62 (6): 741–755.

Bourdieu, Pierre. 1990. *Other Words. Essays Towards a Reflexive Sociology*. Cambridge: Polity Press.

———. 2000. *Pascalian Meditations*. Cambridge: Polity Press.

Bruce, A., C. Lyall, J. Tait, and R. Williams. 2004. Interdisciplinary Integration in the Fifth Framework Programme. *Futures* 36 (4): 457–470.

Buanes, Arild, and Svein Jentoft. 2009. Building Bridges: Institutional Perspectives on Interdisciplinarity. *Futures* 41: 446–454.

Castán Broto, Vanesa, Maya Gislason, and Melf-Hinrich Ehlers. 2009. Practising Interdisciplinarity in the Interplay Between Disciplines: Experiences of Established Researchers. *Environmental Science & Policy* 12 (7): 922–933.

Collini, Stefan. 2012. *What Are Universities for?* London: Penguin.

Collins, Harry, and Robert Evans. 2007. *Rethinking Expertise*. Chicago: Chicago University Press.

Cuevas-Garcia, C.A. 2015. 'I Have Never Cared for Particular Disciplines' – Negotiating an Interdisciplinary Self in Biographical Narrative. *Contemporary Social Science* 10 (1): 86–98.

Cuevas-Garcia, Carlos A. 2016. Sense-Making and Self-Making in Interdisciplinarity: An Analysis of Dilemmatic Discourses of Expertise. PhD Thesis, Technische Universität München.

Eisner, Elliot. 1982. *Cognition and Curriculum: A Basis for Deciding What to Teach*. New York: Longman.

Fam, Dena M., Tanzi Smith, and Dana J. Cordell. 2017. Being a Transdisciplinary Researcher: Skills and Dispositions Fostering Competence in Transdisciplinary Research and Practice. In *Transdisciplinary Research and Practice for Sustainability Outcomes*, ed. D. Fam, J. Palmer, C. Riedy, and C. Mitchell, 122–136. Oxford: Routledge.

Felt, Ulrike, Judith Igelsböck, Andrea Schikowitz, and Thomas Völker. 2012. Growing into What? The (Un-)disciplined Socialisation of Early Stage Researchers in Transdisciplinary Research. *Higher Education* 65 (4): 511–524.

Fischer, E.V., K.R.M. MacKey, et al. 2012. Is Pretenure Interdisciplinary Research a Career Risk. *Eos* 93 (32): 311–312.

Frodeman, Robert. 2014. *Sustainable Knowledge*. Basingstoke: Palgrave.

Hein, Christopher J., John E. Ten Hoeve, Sathya Gopalakrishnan, Ben Livneh, Henry D. Adams, Elizabeth K. Marino, and C. Susan Weiler. 2018. Overcoming Early Career Barriers to Interdisciplinary Climate Change Research. *Wiley Interdisciplinary Reviews: Climate Change* 9 (5): e530.

Hess, Andi. 2018. Two Types of Interdisciplinary Scholarship. *Integration and Implementation Insights*, February 6. https://i2insights.org/2018/02/06/two-types-of-interdisciplinarity/#andi-hess. Accessed 24 January 2019.

Holley, Karri A. 2015. Doctoral Education and the Development of an Interdisciplinary Identity. *Innovations in Education and Teaching International* 52 (6): 642–652.

Kuhn, Thomas S. 1970. *The Structure of Scientific Revolutions*. 2nd ed. Chicago: University of Chicago Press.

Lattuca, Lisa R. 2002. Learning Interdisciplinarity: Sociocultural Perspectives on Academic Work. *The Journal of Higher Education* 73 (6): 711–739.

Lau, Lisa, and Margaret Pasquini. 2008. 'Jack of All Trades'? The Negotiation of Interdisciplinarity Within Geography. *Geoforum* 39 (2): 552–560.

Laudel, Grit, and Jochen Gläser. 2008. From Apprentice to Colleague: The Metamorphosis of Early Career Researchers. *Higher Education* 55 (3): 387–406.

League of European Research Universities. 2016. *Interdisciplinarity and the 21st Century Research-intensive University*. Leuven: LERU.

McBee, D.J., and E. Leahey. 2017. New Directions in Interdisciplinary Training: Trials and Tribulations. In *Investigating Interdisciplinary Research: Theory and Practice Across Disciplines*, ed. B. Prainsack, S. Frickel, and M. Albert. New Brunswick, NJ: Rutgers University Press.

Meagher, L., and C. Lyall. 2009. *Evaluation of ESRC/MRC Interdisciplinary Research Studentship and Post-Doctoral Fellowship Scheme*. Report to ESRC.

Millar, M.M. 2013. Interdisciplinary Research and the Early Career: The Effect of Interdisciplinary Dissertation Research on Career Placement and Publication Productivity of Doctoral Graduates in the Sciences. *Research Policy* 42 (5): 1152–1164.

Nelson, B. 2011. Seeking the Right Toolkit. *Nature* 476: 115–117.

Palmer, Lisa. 2018. Meeting the Leadership Challenges for Interdisciplinary Environmental Research. *Nature Sustainability* 1 (7): 330–333.

Repko, Alan. 2008. *Interdisciplinary Research: Process and Theory*. Los Angeles: Sage.

Rhoten, D., and A. Parker. 2004. Risks and Rewards of an Interdisciplinary Research Path. *Science* 306 (5704): 2046.

Skills Development Scotland. 2018. *Skills 4.0. A Skills Model to Drive Scotland's Future*. Glasgow: Skills Development Scotland.

Strober, Myra H. 2011. *Interdisciplinary Conversations. Challenging Habits of Thought*. Stanford: Stanford University Press.

van der Zwaan, Bert. 2017. *Higher Education in 2040. A Global Approach*. Amsterdam: Amsterdam University Press.

CHAPTER 5

Facilitating Serendipity?

One of the commodities that we value most as academics is time. Alongside an escalating desire to overcome "time poverty" (Berg and Seeber 2016, p. 8), we also cherish "space" (which is "even rarer than money sometimes"— SR2). Awardholders talked about space both in the physical sense of how their working environments affected them as interdisciplinary researchers and they also linked this to lack of time when they spoke about the difficulty of finding "space" in their work schedules to thrive as interdisciplinarians.

This chapter addresses further misalignments within institutions that interviewees characterised as "top down" versus "bottom up" approaches to interdisciplinarity.[1] This, in turn, introduces the idea of "slow research" (Berg and Seeber 2016; Slow Science Academy 2010) and links this to questions about our values and attitudes to risk and of how institutions might facilitate the serendipitous encounters that so often appear to characterise interdisciplinary careers.

Who Drives the Intellectual Agenda?

There were contradictions in my conversations with university leaders about the status of interdisciplinarity within their institutions. The LERU report made it very clear that Vice Rectors of Research would only support

---

[1] This expression arose spontaneously as a result of our discussions about what forms of support their universities offered for interdisciplinary research and was not one that I introduced in the interview questions.

© The Author(s) 2019
C. Lyall, *Being an Interdisciplinary Academic*,
https://doi.org/10.1007/978-3-030-18659-3_5

interdisciplinarity within a clear overarching context of "disciplinary excellence" where "interdisciplinary research does not aim to replace but complement disciplinary research" (LERU 2016, p. 3) and

> [a]cademic institutions that successfully harness the potential of interdisciplinary research and education **while keeping the right balance** [emphasis added] between disciplinarity and interdisciplinarity will be able to reap major benefits. (LERU 2016, p. 4)

This prompted me to ask the university leaders in my sample how they negotiated that balance between inter- and monodisciplinary excellence. This elicited various denials that there was a "balance" or any process of institutional negotiation:

> [W]e are a very bottom up university, our academics are completely free to pursue whatever research they wish. There's absolutely no direction from the top as to any areas that they should work in. (VR2)

This precept of academics being free to do "whatever they want" was reiterated by SR2, despite having opened our conversation with a long description of all the initiatives that her university supported in order to promote interdisciplinary research. Similarly, VR1 talked extensively about the steps her university took to provide "an intellectually driven institutional agenda" that included various initiatives to promote interdisciplinary research but then asserted:

> [T]he balance question therefore we leave really to the individuals. (VR1)

This leadership narrative of academics free to pursue their own research agendas was contested by awardholders who articulated concerns about influence from university management and inappropriate intervention "from the top", describing such "attempts to force contact" (Paterson) as "heavy-handed" (Louisa) and less likely to succeed than bottom up activities:

> [University leaders] are under a lot of pressure from the funding streams, like the GCRF,[2] so that again has motivated the powers-that-be to bring disciplines together. I think sometimes it's difficult to do that from a top down process. (Gina)

[2] Global Challenges Research Fund www.ukri.org/research/global-challenges-research-fund/.

[Y]ou get a top down steer which is bringing together researchers ... there's a kind of surface PR level where it looks very good. But actually how that plays out on the ground I think is really variable and inconsistent. (Norman)

Not all Vice Rectors took such a directive approach. VR2 complained that "levers are quite difficult" while VR3, who had inherited a number of interdisciplinary initiatives from her predecessor that had been created in a fairly top down fashion, asserted that this was not her approach:

I'm not a great fan in general of top down initiatives, particularly for fostering new areas ... I feel I couldn't stay in this building and figure out what should be done. (VR3)

In one case, the loud and soft voices offered contrasting depictions of their university's attempts to foster interdisciplinary dialogue in two interviews, from the same (anonymised) institution:

[W]e have ... general gatherings, and we would come up, say, with a series of actions which are grass roots driven ... I think there's a synergy between bottom up responses to sufficiently well-defined inclusive challenges from a central body. (Anon VR)

[Y]ou attend a lot of ["general gatherings" described above] ... and it's the same people who go around all the new interdisciplinary institute meetings ... that talk about how they can connect their research to this interdisciplinary question and that interdisciplinary question. So it kind of feels a bit like a kind of academic entrepreneurialism from a set of professorial elite ... which looks a bit like a tactical ploy for funding rather than anything particularly substantive. (Anon awardholder)

Intra-institution power dynamics, where the establishment of new interdisciplinary centres by university management became an "issue of control" (SR1), lead to staff feeling threatened by these new centres and prompt concerns that resources were being taken away from their own areas. Moreover, such institutes are often a reincarnation of existing disciplinary structures, rather than entirely new interdisciplinary entities (Rhoten 2004) and can create counterproductive elitism:

[S]tupid barriers being put in place like you couldn't book rooms there unless you were a member of that institute. So I think that meant that other people at the campus haven't engaged with it to the extent that we possibly could or should be doing. (Reuben)

VR5 had a more nuanced understanding of what was required, acknowledging the complexities of "information flow" within the university and of finding ways for the university leadership to recognise and support bottom up approaches in interdisciplinary research:

[N]ot forcing them, for example, people from humanities and natural sciences, to put them together in a meeting and say, you have to find the same language. No. They have only to understand each other and create the problem they want to study. This is the most important thing. (VR5)

So perhaps this is the "balance" I was actually seeking when I spoke to university leaders about their strategies for supporting interdisciplinarity, negotiating the balance between top down and bottom up initiatives:

[I]t has to come from the top to a certain extent but I think the more that those further down the chain play a role in this and kick start these collaborations and conversations, the more likely it is to succeed. (Paterson)

Such success may also be secured by greater recognition of the interdisciplinary expertise that already exists within institutions from those "further down the chain":

[P]eople that have done a joint studentship are so valuable because they have these interdisciplinary networks already … and they know how to bring the right people together who are open-minded to have a conversation about different ways of doing things. I think if you don't have that knowledge, and you're trying to do it from a top down institutional process, you can bring the wrong people together and force it, and I don't think that always works. (Gina)

Other questions of balance undoubtedly exist within a modern university, such as the appropriate mix of research and teaching (van der Zwaan 2017, pp. 24–25) as well as the "optimal balance between efficiency, centralization and size" (ibid., p. 70). On the issue of preserving a balance between disciplinary and interdisciplinary investment, van der Zwaan notes that this will require "careful steering" (ibid., p. 223) and his warning of the risks to the disciplines if research becomes too demand-driven suggests that such "steering" implies delicate navigation rather than the top down push that awardholders were witnessing.

A final form of balance, that between the "new initiative" and recognising and supporting existing strengths, was offered by Owen who epitomised the loud voices' approach to fostering interdisciplinary research and the dominant narrative that persistently links interdisciplinarity with innovation in the shape of new initiatives and institutes at the expense of existing, lower level interdisciplinary activities. University leaders were keen to talk about their multimillion pound building projects in the form of new campuses and flagship institutes but what was missing from these conversations was an appreciation of the softer, informal side of interdisciplinarity.

Informality Is Crucial

The creation of new knowledge is dependent on the interpersonal and "spontaneous interactions" of researchers that are not always facilitated by traditional departments (Rhoten 2004). Making time for "play" (as some might regard forays into interdisciplinarity) can encourage academic creativity:

> [A]fter curiosity led to a compelling problem, and after hard work led to frustration, a decisive advance came while taking a break from the problem into the fun of exploring something new and different. In other words, when the going gets tough, lighten up. (Aldrich 2014, p. 35)

The theme of finding the time and space for informal discussions with colleagues was a persistent one in interviews with awardholders who talked about the importance of frequent, sustained dialogue ("bumping into people from different disciplines, while you're having your coffee", Diana) rather than one-off events ("a workshop here, a sandpit there", Diana). Perhaps senior academics of all complexions inevitably reflect back on the halcyon days of their time as postdocs: Norman recalled his post-doctoral experience as "a wonderful melting pot of ideas" and rued the loss of that institutional culture that promoted "freedom", "proximity to other people" and "the ability just to have a chit chat over coffee, come up with interesting ideas, perspectives that nobody had ever thought of before". Norman's lament was that increasingly, you just lose that time for all those wonderful informal networks, informal discussions that you used to have. I think informality is really crucial to interdisciplinarity. (Norman)

Nowotny (2015, passim.) argues that there should be more scope for scientific freedom and surprise results. One of the themes that emerged from Chap. 2 was the role that chance played in the careers of my sample of awardholders who were reluctant to admit to any overt career strategies and Quentin certainly articulated this very clearly when he claimed his "biggest wins" resulted from "a lot of serendipity".

This raises the further question about whether scholarship is still about trial and error or whether it has been overtaken by planning and prediction in the modern academy. This freedom versus planning dichotomy is not a new debate within science: Pasteur's claim that "chance only favours the mind prepared which is prepared" dates from the mid-nineteenth century[3] and Merton returned to this theme at various points in his writing on serendipity (Merton and Barber 1958; Merton 2004). Starting from the premise that serendipity was a specific individual disposition "a talent for making felicitous discoveries by chance" (ibid., p. 257), Merton concludes that serendipity can be nurtured by "institutional flexibility" (ibid., p. 205) and that "institutionalized serendipity" (ibid., p. 265) is possible in order to foster an interactive and integrative environment.

University leaders acknowledge that an informal approach to implementing the vision of "a virtuous circle between disciplinarity and interdisciplinarity" is possible based on "serendipity" but state that an "integrated strategy" will be needed to make "a significant and lasting impact" (LERU 2016, p. 20). The LERU document notes that interdisciplinarity requires "structures that provide a facilitative and supportive institutional environment" (ibid.) and suggests that

> [a] systemic but non-directive approach is needed to facilitate interactions amongst and between people and structures and ultimately foster an interdisciplinary culture. (LERU 2016, p. 20)

This then raises further questions about *where* interdisciplinary interactions occur and *how* institutional leaders and funders can facilitate this.

---

[3] Vallery-Radot, R. (1920), *The Life of Pasteur* (London, Constable and Company) cited in Merton (2004, p. 163).

A Place to Grow?

The reorganisation of universities may be driven in future by research that takes place in the digital sphere and is much less reliant on physical space and discipline-based structures (van der Zwaan 2017, p. 223) but, for the moment, physical locations that facilitate "serendipitous meetings" that help to create and support a culture of interdisciplinarity are paramount (Aldrich 2014).

The importance of communal spaces and informal meeting points (those "conversations in the corridor") was emphasised time and again by awardholders yet, when space is at a premium, it is these social spaces that are often turned into offices or teaching spaces. Less than a generation ago, universities would have an active university staff club where colleagues would eat together regardless of discipline. Aldrich (2014, p. 55) recounts that such gatherings resulted in a lot of "accidental relationships" and relates an interdisciplinary success that "almost literally required nothing more than lunch to achieve". He does, however, acknowledge (ibid., p. 42) that this required "a supportive institution and the various virtues of the academy such as the ability to expend one's most precious resource, time, pretty much as one sees fit". None of the UK-based universities that I visited seemed to maintain this staff club tradition perhaps as a consequence of growth or, more likely, changing work cultures and increasing time pressures:

> Quite how networking and stuff is supposed to happen, it doesn't even happen in our own department … we don't have the time and space to be able to do that, we're all frantically trying to get everything done. (Belinda)

The disadvantages of universities being situated across multiple campuses, offices remote from the main campus or departments split across two buildings should not be underestimated:

> [I]t's about a ten minute walk but boy does that make a difference … it's not the same thing as popping next door or meeting someone at coffee and being able to discuss your ideas. (Carina)

While there is undoubtedly some truth in the assertion that "so much of academic life can be done on an iPhone wherever you are in the world" (VR2), it is also crucial to be present:

> When I worked ... in the [anon] department, I saw how things happened that didn't necessarily get circulated on emails, there's a lot of other stuff going on that, if you weren't there, you wouldn't know was happening. (Erica)

Many fellow academics will recognise the reality of Quentin's working experience:

> [T]his building I'm sat in now, it's a building that's been designed without corridors and the only communal areas have PhD students in so you are not allowed to talk. Now, there is a massive body of literature showing how all the creativity happens in corridors and around water coolers. And we've just built a building with neither. It's bizarre. (Quentin)

While VR2 was vocal in her criticism of the practicalities of providing staff with offices in different campus locations, interdisciplinarians need that "place to grow", flexible spaces where "exploration and conversation are as valued as collaboration" (Lattuca 2001, pp. 259–260).

University leaders and funding agencies should not underrate the role of the built environment in fostering collective behaviour and enhancing collaboration (Pinter-Wollman et al. 2018; Dzeng 2013). But this then raises another important aspect of "balance". Some argue that interdisciplinary research needs its own "neutral space" (Veronica Strang quoted in Reisz 2018) but this risks "othering" interdisciplinarity (Lindvig 2017, pp. 28–30) where interdisciplinary research is treated differently from other "normal" practices. This, in turn, presents similar hazards and associated career drawbacks to interdisciplinary research centres as discussed in Chap. 3.

Facilitating the Small Stuff

It was surely significant that, during my conversation with Paterson, he could not recall which group he was now part of following an institutional reorganisation intended to foster collaboration:

> [F]or me, it's always felt like the environment and structures are kind of less important. To me, it's about myself and who I get to know and who I like to work with and who would like to work with me, those kind of bottom up networks that I've created is probably the most important thing arguably rather than sort of the structure I find myself in. (Paterson)

Such personal networks

- are enduring ("You can look up experts in your department but it's nowhere near the same as knowing that that was the person I sat next to when I did my PhD", Carina)
- arise through unexpected routes (e.g. Louisa's meetings with new colleagues on the picket line[4])
- require creativity (Anna) and personal responsibility (Una)
- need mutually respectful spaces where "anything goes" and "it's fine if you don't understand something" (Vera)

For Quentin, the best thing about his time in Sweden was "fika":

[E]very single day between 11 and 12, there's a room with coffee and cake in it and everyone goes and just hangs out and chats and it's amazing. And you know what? They don't have any meetings as a result. It was just phenomenal. The meetings happened there. So the head of department would often just stand up and say, I've got a few announcements. Job done. No emails, no meetings. Plus all that networking. (Quentin)

However, VR1 was dismissive of my suggestion that what colleagues crave is the time and the space and appropriate meeting places to facilitate those informal, serendipitous encounters that awardholders regarded as crucial to their success as interdisciplinarians:

I think that's a soft argument personally … "wouldn't it be nice to be able to have a chat over a cup of coffee". What we have [at the core of her university's flagship interdisciplinary activity], we have an executive group and, in order to be on the executive group, you have to deliver something at the end of the day. (VR1)

Quentin talked about work/life balance and increasing university workloads, relaying advice that he had been given to "stop doing all the small stuff, stop doing the unimportant stuff". The "important stuff" according to Quentin's university managers was applying for large grants but Quentin's riposte to this was

---

[4] At the time that interviews were taking place in the UK, members of the University and College Union were taking strike action in protest at changes to their pension scheme.

that would be fine if I could predict the future because, guess what ... I don't spend time writing proposals knowing they're going to fail. Or meeting people knowing that we're not going ever do anything together. The good stuff comes from all these little things that often seem pointless at the time. (Quentin)

Quentin alluded to the "strength of weak ties" (Granovetter 1973):

[I]t's not exactly obscure stuff, you know about innovation and where it comes from and trying to create lots of weak ties across different networks, trying to maintain lots of different networks. There is actually theory behind this stuff and it flies in the face of what we're told to do, which is target the topics everyone else is working on, target the big funding schemes that everyone else is targeting, target the top 10 journals that everyone else is targeting. (Quentin)

These weak ties are characterised as "indispensable to individuals' opportunities and to their integration into communities" (Granovetter 1973) in contrast to strong ties, which encourage local cohesion but ultimately lead to fragmentation. In other words, strong ties are likely to foster cliques (as one might define a discipline), whereas weak ties are more likely to connect members to a breadth of different groups.

The misalignment between the loud and soft voices suggests that university leaders are trying to foster strong interdisciplinary ties through the formation of top down interdisciplinary institutes and initiatives, whereas the soft voices are striving for ways to establish weaker links through often serendipitous engagements with other colleagues elsewhere in the university so that they then develop their own research collaborations. So the question then is how do universities, which are increasingly driven by income generation and accountability, foster such weak ties: is it possible to facilitate serendipity?

INTERDISCIPLINARY RESEARCH AS SLOW RESEARCH

Stirling et al. (2018) urge us to resist the pressures of modern academia and describe interdisciplinary (or, in their case, transdisciplinary) encounters with non-academic research partners as a form of "slow knowledge" where these projects are not just "one-off" but reflect relationships sustained over time.

It is generally recognised that interdisciplinary research usually takes longer to produce results because, inter alia, of the extra time needed to access new literature, learn new concepts and perhaps build and foster dialogue within a new research team. Leahey et al. (2017) have shown numerically that this slowness contributes to a "productivity penalty" where interdisciplinary scholars gain greater prominence through citations but are less productive than their monodisciplinary peers with their publication output.

Helena described her career as "a marathon and not a sprint" and talked about the advantages of a slow career. While she recognised that some of her contemporaries were further on in their careers, she saw this as a benefit as it expanded her personal networks to include colleagues across a range of career stages. Other awardholders talked more broadly about interdisciplinary research being slow research, for example:

> [Y]ou can't have that kind of rapid turnover of research which I think you can when you work in a very narrow sub disciplinary field ... interdisciplinary scholarship is slower ... that's really important to realise and appreciate. (Norman)

They also talked about careers going in cycles where, at some points, we focus more on grant applications or we go through periods where we focus more on teaching, for example:

> You can't always be in the policy room, you can't always be in the deliberative space where you're trying to get these conversations going with the public. I do all of that stuff but I find it goes in cycles where you have to come back and reflect and write things up and push forward—you have to have time to read and I don't think you can do everything all the time. Well, certainly you can't do it well if you do everything all the time. So there is a bit of a juggling act that comes with it. (Tristan)

These cycles can be longer for interdisciplinary research so, if we recognise the cyclical nature of research and interdisciplinary research in particular, how do we allow for these cycles; must they always be fitted around a rigid sabbatical schedule?

The Slow Science Manifesto (Slow Science Academy 2010) calls for time to "misunderstand each other, especially when fostering lost dialogue between humanities and natural sciences" and points out that science needs "time to fail". If contemporary academic life is indeed typified by "distractedness and fragmentation" (Berg and Seeber 2016, p. 90) what does this mean for interdisciplinary integration, which by Orr's definition, is the very opposite of fast knowledge:

> Fast knowledge is mostly linear; slow knowledge is complex and ecological. (Orr 2002, p. 40)

Interdisciplinarity as a form of "slow scholarship" is of course antithetical to what many see as the recent neo-liberal reforms of universities with their focus on increased specialisation, commercialisation and accountability (Bergland 2017):

> One of the downsides of contemporary universities is that you're so fixated on delivering the teaching target for your department or delivering on whatever the grant proposal thing is that you've got to deliver. (Norman)

Van der Zwaan (2017, p. 75) stresses that universities are not truly commercial entities and tend to thrive when academic freedom is respected within "relatively small communities". Others call for a "feminist ethics of care", as epitomised by slow scholarship, where we "[c]ount what others don't" and acknowledge more fully the contributions to the academy of activities such as community building and mentoring and supporting our students and colleagues (Mountz et al. 2015).

A problem for everyone but especially those who work part-time or have family commitments or long commutes, networking is always the activity that gets squeezed out of a busy day. This introduces an additional problem for interdisciplinary researchers:

> [T]he important thing is to have a series of public events in the institution which are addressing a variety of questions. I mean, there are lots and lots of things going on [at this university] where you can go at 5 o'clock and listen to a lecture. The biggest problem might be providing that with a family friendly agenda because often cross-disciplinary falls outside the normal hours. (VR1)

Why must we accept that "cross-disciplinary falls outside the normal hours"? This speaks to what our institutions value and echoes the perception of interdisciplinary research as "other" as noted above or a "sideline" (see Chap. 4).

This sense of the value that we ascribe to what we might regard as "slow research" was underscored by awardholders:

> I suppose the institution doesn't encourage you to have a lot of free time because we all work so much. So in that sense, [interdisciplinarity] is not encouraged because everyone is drowning in work. (Louisa)

> [I]t depends how seriously [university leaders] want to take this and I would imagine not seriously enough that they, for example, would take off something from your workload in order to really get departments talking and communicating, which takes time and effort and energy and money. (Paterson)

Not only does it require time and space to network informally, it also requires a general acceptance that the majority of these interactions may not lead anywhere. I recall a memorable remark from a colleague at Edinburgh that being successful at interdisciplinary research meant "being in the right place at the right time" but in order to do that you needed to be "in lots of different places a lot of the time". Only one of the Vice Rectors acknowledged that such networking or pilot activities might fail. This ran contrary to the broader assumption with other research leaders that seed money for interdisciplinary activities would lead to grant income. This is significant in an environment where everything is becoming accountable and hard choices have to be made:

> [E]verybody has a choice about how they spend time ... How you choose to use that time ... is the question that each of us has to address ... if I'm interested in a question that requires an interdisciplinary approach, I will have to make contacts and learn something about other fields. That's going to take time. How long can I afford to do that and gestate a project before it yields some outcome, when that outcome may also be a little bit uncertain ... that is a challenging set of questions when there's [a project that] fits in with a currently funded area of research, I know I can get funding, I know I'm going be able to publish something in it, and that's going to be critical for my future ... One has to be thinking about—in my research portfolio, what's going to be the things that I can get some immediate return from and what's the long term investment I think I need. (VR4)

Yet "[n]ot everything that counts can be counted" (Collini 2012, p. 120) and academics, at all stages but most especially early career researchers, would benefit from better advice on how to achieve this balanced portfolio that VR4 is promulgating. This is not simply about time management training or managing your inbox; it is about how to be a successful academic and I return to this theme of academic career mentoring in the following chapter.

This chapter has discussed the need for balance in several aspects of academic life. There is an inherent hypocrisy in university leaders, research funders and policymakers claiming that they want to facilitate interdisciplinarity and then not creating the conditions that the experienced interdisciplinarians whom I interviewed say they need in order to foster this style of working. The counter argument to the sceptics who want to get "the right balance" between interdisciplinary research and disciplinary excellence is that fostering the conditions that will allow interdisciplinarity to blossom will also be good for research that stays within one discipline. There is a certain consensus in the literature and among my awardholder interviewees that sustainable interdisciplinary research is rooted in researcher-led "bottom up" approaches (e.g. Aldrich 2014) and that funding agencies should support such approaches "despite the potential risks associated with the most innovative ideas" (Gleed and Marchant 2016). In particular, funders have been urged to facilitate the design of physical and social spaces to foster the development of interdisciplinary working (Gleed and Marchant 2016) but this will require some radical rethinking of how we manage both our time and space—and ultimately what we value about the academy—within traditional university structures.

Talking Points
While institutional strategies may appear to favour interdisciplinarity, such high-level statements may not be enacted in ways that support the actual experiences of would-be interdisciplinary researchers. Informal networks, shared physical spaces, and attention to personal relationships and soft skills all play a role but are often overlooked by institutions.

Who—and what—drives the intellectual agenda for interdisciplinary research within our universities? As a community, can we create opportunities to step back and think through issues and processes related to the generation of high-quality interdisciplinary research?

If interdisciplinarity is characterised by "slowness", what implications could that have for career choice given different institutional environments (e.g. interdisciplinary research centre vs. traditional university department)? How do researchers who are striving for ways to establish more meaningful interdisciplinary research engagements, (often through less structured, serendipitous encounters) avoid becoming an anathema in the modern academy?

References

Aldrich, John. 2014. *Interdisciplinarity*. Oxford: Oxford University Press.

Berg, Maggie, and Barbara K. Seeber. 2016. *The Slow Professor. Challenging the Culture of Speed in the Academy*. Toronto: University of Toronto Press.

Bergland, Brita. 2017. The Incompatibility of Neoliberal University Structures and Interdisciplinary Knowledge: A Feminist Slow Scholarship Critique. *Educational Philosophy and Theory* 50 (11): 1031–1036.

Collini, Stefan. 2012. *What Are Universities for?* London: Penguin.

Dzeng, Elizabeth. 2013. How to Inspire Interdisciplinarity: Lessons from the Collegiate System. *The Guardian*, March 15.

Gleed, A, and D. Marchant. 2016. Interdisciplinarity. Survey Report for the Global Research Council 2016 Annual Meeting, Stockport.

Granovetter, Mark S. 1973. The Strength of Weak Ties. *American Journal of Sociology* 78 (6): 1360–1380.

Lattuca, Lisa R. 2001. *Creating Interdisciplinarity*. Nashville: Vanderbilt University Press.

League of European Research Universities. 2016. *Interdisciplinarity and the 21st Century Research-Intensive University*. Leuven: LERU.

Leahey, E., C.M. Beckman, and T.L. Stanko. 2017. Prominent but Less Productive: The Impact of Interdisciplinarity on Scientists' Research. *Administrative Science Quarterly* 62 (1): 105–139.

Lindvig, Katrine. 2017. Creating Interdisciplinarity Within Monodisciplinary Structures. PhD Thesis, University of Copenhagen.

Merton, R.K. 2004. Afterword. Autobiographical Reflections on the Travels and Adventures of Serendipity. In *The Travels and Adventures of Serendipity: A Study in Sociological Semantics and the Sociology of Science*, ed. R.K. Merton and E. Barber. Princeton: Princeton University Press.

Merton, R., and E. Barber. 1958. *The Travels and Adventures of Serendipity*. Princeton: Princeton University Press.

Mountz, Alison, et al. 2015. For Slow Scholarship: A Feminist Politics of Resistance Through Collective Action in the Neoliberal University. *ACME: An International E-Journal for Critical Geographies* 14 (4): 1235–1259.

Nowotny, Helga. 2015. *The Cunning of Uncertainty*. Cambridge: Polity Press.

Orr, David W. 2002. *Nature of Design: Ecology, Culture, and Human Intention*. Oxford: Oxford University Press.

Pinter-Wollman, N., A. Penn, G. Theraulaz, and S.M. Fiore. 2018. Interdisciplinary Approaches for Uncovering the Impacts of Architecture on Collective Behaviour. *Philosophical Transactions of the Royal Society B: Biological Sciences* 373 (1753).

Reisz, Matthew. 2018. Interdisciplinarity and Global View 'Priorities for Humanities'. *Times Higher Education*, January 20.

Rhoten, Diana. 2004. Interdisciplinary Research: Trend or Transition. *Items and Issues* 5 (1–2): 6–11.

Slow Science Academy. 2010. The Slow Science Manifesto. Slow-science.org. Accessed 24 January 2019.

Stirling, Andy, Adrian Ely, and Fiona Marshall. 2018. How Is Transformative Knowledge 'Coproduced'? I2S blog. https://i2insights.org/2018/04/03/co-producing-transformative-knowledge/. Accessed 24 January 2019.

van der Zwaan, Bert. 2017. *Higher Education in 2040. A Global Approach*. Amsterdam: Amsterdam University Press.

CHAPTER 6

Towards New Logics of Interdisciplinarity

RECONCEPTUALISING INTERDISCIPLINARY SCHOLARSHIP

Interdisciplinarity undoubtedly presents an organisational problem for universities (Weingart 2014, p. 7). This mode of research is promoted but is by no means systemic within the governance of universities. Previous chapters have analysed the conflicting rhetorics between, on the one hand, interdisciplinarity that seeks to cross boundaries, synthesise knowledge sources and embrace broader skill sets and, on the other hand, traditional academia with its discipline focus and emphasis on in-depth knowledge and specialisation. Throughout this book we have heard the mantra of disciplinary excellence that characterises research-led universities. Despite the prevalence of the interdisciplinary rhetoric within their institutions and from their funders, the conversations I had with both awardholders and research leaders indicated that the ethos within their universities is one where the hegemony of disciplines triumphs and interdisciplinarity still risks being seen as "too soft for real tough minds" (Weingart 2000, p. 29). I want to expand this conception of academic scholarly excellence in the context of the twenty-first-century university to incorporate a better understanding of *interdisciplinary* excellence into this academic credo in order to address the conflicting rhetorics and provide firmer foundations for interdisciplinary careers within UK universities.

In this penultimate chapter, I therefore identify two new principles that should underpin the development of a successful interdisciplinary environment. These principles build on a series of rationales or "logics" that have

© The Author(s) 2019
C. Lyall, *Being an Interdisciplinary Academic*,
https://doi.org/10.1007/978-3-030-18659-3_6

previously been proposed to guide interdisciplinary, first by Barry et al. (2008) and then adopted and adapted by others (e.g. Callard et al. 2015; Fitzgerald et al. 2014; Van der Hel 2016). Such logics condition (both positively and negatively) the behaviours of actors operating within institutions.

First, there is the logic of intention. If institutions are going to embark on a successful strategy of fostering interdisciplinarity, there must be clarity of purpose. Secondly, there is the logic of commitment: if institutions are to develop effective interdisciplinarity, this requires a whole-institution approach in order to overcome the many academic and administrative barriers that exist.

The dichotomy between "specialists" and "generalists" is a potent issue in the debate about how institutions regard interdisciplinarity. Interdisciplinary boundary crossers may be perceived as being guilty of "disciplinary tourism" (Mills 2010, p. 71), giving rise to qualms about research quality. Quentin—who "hated to be pigeon-holed"—had never been attracted towards being a specialist:

> I can't think of anything worse, it's just boring and you miss most of what's interesting in the world. But of course, a lot of academia is set up so that you need to look like you're a specialist in something. Every single mentoring meeting or career guidance meeting I've ever had, people have said, you need to stop doing so much, you need to just pick one thing and become a specialist. And I have resolutely refused to do that. (Quentin)

This attitude had not prevented Quentin from achieving a professorship but he did concede that, as a result, he had tended to specialise more in methodologies (both for academic knowledge production or methods for different modes of partnering to produce knowledge from non-academic partners).

If we learn to see beyond advances in a single discipline as the sole marker of excellence, we will extend the image of the traditional academic and recognise that "[g]roundbreaking achievements take many forms" (Benson et al. 2016):

> [W]hat's worked well in the geography department is that … the criteria by which we judge each other … have been adapted somewhat. We're not all expected to get *Nature* and *Science* papers and also not all expected to write a single-authored monograph, so there's somewhere in between that interdisciplinary researchers can still show that they are producing valid outputs. (Fiona)

VR1 used a very revealing phrase when talking about her university's flagship interdisciplinary initiative:

> First meeting, pontificated, they just talked about what they knew. Second meeting, they did that again. Third meeting, *we started to share ignorance* [emphasis added] and it was that beginning of a collegial sense of trust and [that] enabled them to reveal their weaknesses, which is quite unusual in alpha academics. And they then started to find the questions and it was then that the rubber hit the road. (VR1)

This willingness to be vulnerable lies at the heart of the interdisciplinary character but "alpha academics" are typically reluctant to admit that they are not experts. Universities are often strongly traditional establishments[1] where staff are more usually rewarded for individual achievements than team efforts. Ironically, given that a raison d'être for universities is ostensibly to discover new things and encourage innovation (VR7), research leaders acknowledged the slow pace of change:

> [I]nternational excellence of universities is measured in a certain way and we're not going to be able to change that overnight. So we need to make sure we can work within that framework. (VR4)

Notwithstanding interdisciplinary experience spanning NGO, policy and academic roles in several countries, Gina's expertise was not recognised when her university set up new interdisciplinary research centres. Instead, people were selected to lead these interdisciplinary centres on the basis of "good" publications and not as a consequence of their practical expertise and dispositions.

Although academia is seen as an internationally mobile career, listening to Fiona discussing her career transitions—between countries and field sites and from a research-only institute to a full spectrum university—also confirms that universities can be very conservative in appreciating prior knowledge. I recognise this from my own experience when, as a late entrant to a university career, I was reminded by a professor that I was still quite junior as I was only a few years past my PhD. This despite being in my 40s at the time, with a professional career behind me. Likewise Helena, who was trailblazing a career that straddled two worlds between the NHS

---

[1] Especially, one might suggest, those within the LERU and Russell mission groups that formed the core of my sample.

and her university, also made me consider that universities could do much more to accommodate the "non-traditional career" and adjust their metrics accordingly, focusing less on "academic age".[2]

Iona's description of a job interview, where there was reluctance to employ someone who "wasn't a pure psychologist" similarly illustrates the very conventional views of academic recruiters which Louisa had witnessed from the other side of the recruitment panel, admitting that her department would not even look at "non standard" CVs. Although supportive of interdisciplinary academic careers, VR3 admitted, somewhat ironically, that she did not get involved in recruitment which went through the "more traditional" departmental and deanery structures. Even though universities might look for people with "expertise in non-standard spaces", the view prevails that universities appoint staff who can teach "the basics" (VR1). We noted this in our original evaluations of these studentship schemes (Meagher and Lyall 2005, 2009) and this remained a concern among awardholders, as we saw in Chap. 3.

Others had a slightly different interpretation of the expertise issue and associated this with problems with job hunting for positions outside of academia because, compared with other workplaces, universities were seen to be slow at giving staff responsibility ("you've got a certain title, therefore this is what you can do and you can't really do anything more", Mariana). When I talked to Mariana about her skills, I suggested that, as an interdisciplinary researcher who could bridge different disciplines, she brought additional skills as an integrator or an interpreter but she contended that such skills were only recognised at more senior staff grades and not at the post-doctoral level. Concerns that research staff are not recognised for the skills they have are echoed by Sobey et al. (2013) who identified such colleagues as "an underused resource within multidisciplinary [sic] research as most networking opportunities are found at higher levels". Yet, we have also found that the all-important co-ordinator or facilitator role in interdisciplinary collaborations frequently falls to a relatively junior (and often female) member of the team (Meagher and Lyall 2005, 2013).[3]

---

[2] See, for example, Dorothy Hodgkin Fellowship https://royalsociety.org/grants-schemes-awards/grants/dorothy-hodgkin-fellowship/ (accessed 12/1/19).

[3] Factor in the finding that, in mixed research groups, males may be perceived to contribute more than females (Lerchenmueller and Sorenson 2018) who undertake more than their fair share of these "housekeeping roles" that often underpin success in interdisciplinary research and this then begins to introduce an important gender dimension where women in

My overarching impression from these interviews is that universities still take a very traditional stance on what an academic career path looks like; one that does not fully recognise and capitalise upon the different talents and skills of those who have followed a more interdisciplinary route. At a time when universities are losing their monopoly on knowledge production (Frodeman 2014) and are being forced to adapt in order to produce the people and research that society wants (Foray and Sors 2014), institutions that aspire to succeed as interdisciplinary centres of excellence will be obliged to adopt a more encompassing understanding of the qualities that make a "good" academic career.

These observations compel institutions to rethink what we mean by specialist, not just in terms of the "disciplinary excellence" that Vice Rectors talked about, but the other "meta" skills that interdisciplinary researchers possess such as leadership, communication, negotiation and so on (e.g. Skills Development Scotland 2018). Interviewees (e.g. Vera) spoke about the advantages of the breadth and creative linkages that such individuals can bring as complements to disciplinary depth, stressing the benefits to avoiding the appointment of academic "clones" (VR3, see also Chap. 4), and the importance of institutional diversity with respect to culture and gender, recognising that "interdisciplinarity is part of that diversity" (SR1).

Interdisciplinarians are not failed disciplinarians and such "generalists" (an often disparaging term) should not be seen as second-tier academics. This calls for more permeable boundaries both between disciplines and between careers inside and outside of academia. This is especially true in the era of impact[4] where more diverse professional skills and networks can be a substantial benefit and organisations that are diverse and flexible can adapt and thrive.

LOGIC OF INTENTION

When I asked VR3 what advice she would give to other universities that wanted to support interdisciplinarity, she said it would be "to try and not make it look unusual". This was the Vice Rector who described interdisci-

---

interdisciplinary research may be doubly disadvantaged (Rhoten and Pfirman 2007), a topic that clearly warrants further investigation but is beyond the scope of this current work.

[4] The relationship between interdisciplinarity and impact was a significant topic in my interviews with awardholders and one that I have decided to address in a separate publication.

plinarity as being "baked in" to her university's research strategy and who thought an interdisciplinary approach was acceptable at any stage of an academic career. In marked contrast, SR2 was "not sure if we should support it". This contradicted what she had proudly told me at the start of the interview about the initiatives that her university used to encourage interdisciplinary research, in a typical example of the dissonances that characterised so many of these conversations.

VR1's description of her university's activities to promote interdisciplinary engagements resonated with the "othering" of interdisciplinarity (Lindvig 2017, see Chap. 4) where interdisciplinary work is separated out from "normal" activities. This reinforced observations from other interviewees (e.g. Gina, Norman, Reuben) about the sense of elitism or inequitable distribution of resources that this othering can engender, for example, when universities establish new "interdisciplinary" institutes.

Other research leaders occupied a middle ground, embracing what I termed the "excellence with sensitisation" model advocating gradual exposure to interdisciplinarity from undergraduate studies onwards (e.g. VR6). But, as discussed in Chap. 4, this approach belies the tacit differences between disciplines that cannot readily be understood simply through sensitisation.

Lindvig and Hillersdal (2018) develop this theme in their study of one university's attempts to introduce an interdisciplinary research culture where ambiguous goals resulted in uneven implementation and ultimately replicated monodisciplinary research and power structures meaning that genuine interdisciplinary engagement, although much vaunted, was superficial at best.

Such inconstancy features widely in university strategies where interdisciplinarity is promulgated but not adequately acknowledged as mainstream or "legitimate work" and where clarity of purpose and alignment with academic incentive structures are "necessary but unmet conditions for fostering and promoting interdisciplinarity throughout the university" (Razzaq et al. 2013). Institutional reorganisations come with "transaction costs" relating to entrenched governance structures and organisational cultures antithetical to interdisciplinary ways of working that cannot be tackled by "episodic financial incentives" alone (Sá 2008). Instead, this calls for greater recognition and consistency within institutions and incentive structures in which academic rigour is not solely equated with disciplinary excellence (Bergland 2017):

> [R]ecognition that actually being interdisciplinarity is OK ...sometimes interdisciplinarity is seen as a great thing, sometimes it's seen as a bit of a derogatory thing ... Not say, oh it's great to have lots of money coming in from this interdisciplinary proposal but we can't understand what you do, or we can't recognise you for the work that you do. (Vera)

Mixed messages about the position of interdisciplinarity within our institutions indeed prosper. In Chap. 3, I highlighted the predominant policy links made between innovation and interdisciplinarity (the "logic of innovation", Barry et al. 2008) and how this is currently reflected in the powerful research funding drivers in the UK. Research leaders (e.g. VR2, VR4, VR6) were concerned that interdisciplinary research should not be seen as "a goal in itself" but that the motivation should be "to do good research on important projects" but none of the awardholders whom I interviewed had implied that they took an interdisciplinary approach simply for the sake of it, or because that was where the funding was (why would they, given the generally recognised career disadvantages?). The fact that the research leaders felt the need to emphasise this point underlines a tension: "[S]ometimes in discussions about interdisciplinary research, it's about the disciplines and not about the research" (VR7).

In Chap. 4, I introduced Berlin's (1953) division of scholars into two categories and asked whether, in order to build resilient research communities for the twenty-first century and beyond, we aim for more interdisciplinary "foxes" or monodisciplinary "hedgehogs". The answer, of course, is that successful research institutions require both approaches but research leaders must be much clearer about their intentions in promoting interdisciplinarity and deliver a consistent message about its value and appreciation in order to create parity of opportunity for both the hedgehogs and the foxes within our universities.

Logic of Commitment

Interdisciplinarity remains subject to a "mix of enthusiasm and advocacy alongside scepticism and caution" (Winskel 2018) such that interdisciplinary research is "unevenly institutionalised" (Klein and Falk-Krzesinski 2017). The "sense of safety in disciplines" (Gulbenkian Commission 1996, p. 97) still gives reassurance.

Universities were urged to think carefully about their structures and procedures before promoting interdisciplinary training:

> [W]hat career pathway are they encouraging with that kind of interdisciplinary research? What would that PhD student come out with and what are that student's job prospects afterwards? Would that student be able to continue in that university or is that university promoting those type of PhDs but then not providing openings and opportunities within their own departments for people like that? …How can they help promote their careers and how can they be maybe more open to those types of people? (Mariana)

This strongly echoes our recommendations when we evaluated these schemes (Meagher and Lyall 2005) that what was required was a comprehensive interdisciplinary career pathway. Yet, nearly 15 years later, funders are still not recognising the potential pitfalls that their funding focus might create. Others did take a more systemic approach, recognising the challenge of providing follow through and not simply paying "lip service" to interdisciplinary research without providing adequate structures and that these issues reached beyond the university:

> [W]e want to stimulate [interdisciplinary research] because we think the system not only within the university but also the publication channels, the education of students, careers … the main focus is still on the disciplinary path and publication outcomes and so on. So that's why we chose to stimulate it. (VR7)

But, in general, the research leaders whom I interviewed did not express this holistic level of institutional commitment. Successful interdisciplinary careers require a whole-institution approach, recognising that there are also broader governance issues in play (such as publication processes) and that funders also bear responsibility when their funding priorities drive careers in a specific direction. In the next section, I propose a series of steps that institutions could take in order to affirm their commitment to interdisciplinary careers.

MOVING FORWARD WITH INTERDISCIPLINARITY

Promotion and Reward Structures

While there is ample evidence in the literature of the deterrents to interdisciplinarity (e.g. Blackmore and Kandiko 2011) and the cultural and organisational changes required to address these (e.g. Holley 2009), "the gap between the rhetoric of endorsement and the reality of practice" endures (Klein et al. 2016). Nowhere is this more evident than in university promotion criteria, which are persistently ranked as the highest impediment to interdisciplinary work (e.g. NAS 2005; Tarrant and Thiele 2017), and the reality remains that

> [f]oundations may give grants to imaginative groups of scholars but departments decide on promotions or course curricula (Gulbenkian Commission 1996, p. 97)

I asked awardholders and research leaders whether their institution offered any specific guidance regarding promotion and progression for those who follow a more interdisciplinary route. Terms such as "opaque", "lack of transparency", "generic" and "based on patronage" were used in conversations about universities' promotion processes. While some did describe a promotions and appraisals process that explicitly valued non-standard academic characteristics (VR1) and a process of "educating" promotion panels, so that they were open to considering an interdisciplinary CV "in the right way" (VR7), others (e.g. Fiona) described a metricised basis to promotions with set targets for numbers of publications or amount of grant income. More hearteningly, some interviewees noted updates and revisions to procedures but felt there was still some way to go, describing, for example, a lack of parity in promotion procedures between and within departments (Belinda, Diana). Interviewees called on universities to not just "talk the talk" (Tristan) but to "put their money where their mouth is" (Helena) with respect to promotion procedures, with

> a system for recognising … what value the interdisciplinary contribution has towards the recognition of merit as an academic. … explaining what interdisciplinary might mean in terms of outputs related to a person's … academic standing. (Vera)

Reflecting back on the suggestion that interdisciplinary research is often "slow research" (see Chap. 5), the point was made that university procedures do not adequately acknowledge that, in the early stages, new interdisciplinary collaborations can take longer to establish:

> Within the kind of promotion criteria and the kind of indicators of success … thinking about research grant success and papers that you've written, the criteria that we see here at [current university] at least, there's no mention of interdisciplinarity in there and so if you're expecting X number of papers or number of research proposals, then … that has to be in there somewhere. (Owen)

While there is excellent material on this subject originating from the US (notably Klein 2010; Klein et al. 2016) there is no equivalent of the formal tenure process in UK universities around which much of the discussion of interdisciplinary careers in the US hinges and consequently much less career guidance available for UK academics and their institutional leaders.

The University of Edinburgh has been pioneering this area. In 2015, we developed guidance[5] on the consideration of interdisciplinary careers as part of the university's promotion documentation, updating this in 2017 to incorporate additional guidance for assessment of team researchers who may or may not be working in interdisciplinary teams (so-called team science[6]). This publicly accessible document aims to assist both colleagues preparing a case for promotion and those evaluating such cases as members of promotion panels. It outlines ways in which levels of quality can be assessed appropriately and fairly and highlights some of the characteristics and acknowledged difficulties of assessing individual contributions to research activity when individuals are working across traditional discipline boundaries.

Role Models, Mentors and Champions

If we are committed to the advancement of interdisciplinary careers how can we best achieve this? Reward and recognition systems are pivotal but this is not the whole story. A system-wide approach that spans the whole career life cycle and recognises that it is not as simple as "fixing" the promotion rules (Klein and Falk-Krzesinski 2017) is called for. For example, Graybill et al. (2006) call for advice and support in how to develop professional identities, juggle multiple commitments and present their skill sets to future employers and discuss how these are equally essential to an interdisciplinary post-doctoral researcher as the training they typically receive from PIs in the disciplinary requirements of their research projects.

The importance of mentors and role models in providing advice and creating the right environment for interdisciplinarity to thrive was highlighted by awardholders (e.g. Carina, Erica, Norman) while others (e.g. Diana, Katya) spoke specifically about the importance of having a mentor who was independent from the supervisory or line management team.

---

[5] www.ed.ac.uk/files/atoms/files/guidance_on_interdisciplinary_and_team_research_2018.pdf (accessed 05/06/19).

[6] www.acmedsci.ac.uk/policy/policy-projects/team-science (accessed 12/01/19).

Others were less fortunate: Louisa had not experienced mentoring and the staff annual progress reviews "often don't happen unless someone insists on them" while in Quentin's case he had sought mentoring informally as his university (along with others in the data set) appeared to conflate mentoring unhelpfully with staff annual review.

A generational issue hinders developments here: Fiona asserted that effective mentors truly understand the nuances of interdisciplinarity but felt that this was less common at the higher levels of academic leadership or management where there may be fewer advanced interdisciplinary researchers to serve as role models.

If a university were to establish such a mentoring scheme, there is a risk that it might place too great a reliance on certain experienced individuals. An alternative would be to develop national networks of interdisciplinary mentors through funding bodies or professional organisations such as learned academies. Interdisciplinary scholars may also benefit from multiple mentors across different disciplines or consider "non-traditional" mentors (Fischer et al. 2012).

On this question of role models, the LERU (2016) report debated whether institutions should appoint interdisciplinary "champions" at the level of Vice Rector. From my conversations with a sample of these Vice Rectors, it was evident that they did not welcome this suggestion. Nevertheless, what I did discern in some of these research leader interviews was a lack of nuanced appreciation of what interdisciplinary research might constitute within the arts, humanities and social sciences compared with interdisciplinarity within the natural and medical sciences. As noted before, from conversations with Gina and Julia, it was also evident that their universities did not maximise the potential of capitalising on the interdisciplinary expertise of their own staff. So perhaps rather than the high-level "interdisciplinary champion" mooted by the authors of the LERU report, a more effective strategy would be a network of champions or "super mentors" at different levels of university governance who could advise and coach staff to demonstrate consistent support and commitment to interdisciplinary careers.

One of the mechanisms suggested in interviews with supervisors as part of the evaluation of the original studentship schemes (Meagher and Lyall 2005, p. 36) was "streamlining internal university procedures (e.g. registry), including perhaps the appointment of a senior official of the university with responsibility for interdisciplinarity university-wide". Martin and Pfirman (2017) recommend something similar either in the form of an administrative committee or individual. So perhaps what is also apposite is a senior figure to act rather like an interdisciplinary ombudsman to ensure that university processes provide consistent and fair treatment of staff who work in an interdisciplinary way.

Support for Early Career Researchers

Mentoring is only one aspect of good academic support for early career researchers. Hein et al.'s (2018) survey identified a training gap in, for example, communication and team skills along with a demand for greater networking opportunities with other interdisciplinary scholars to "leverage confidence". This sense of community building was precisely what we recommended to the Research Councils when we evaluated these interdisciplinary studentship schemes (Meagher and Lyall 2005), as it was evident that many of those studentship awardholders were adrift and floundering.

Erica knew that publications were required in order to progress but pointed to poor researcher development support and how this varied between departments within the same university:

> I never really know what you can and can't do … when I worked in the [medical department] … that was very different. They didn't care about your personal [development], they cared about the project. They were not interested in you having a few hours off to go to a talk, you had to ask permission, whereas it's very relaxed in the [social science] department. (Erica)

I asked research leaders if they provided support for early career researchers who follow an interdisciplinary route. Research support in the sense of assistance with grant applications is relatively commonplace but is much less likely to be tailored for interdisciplinary research. Publicity from SR2's university depicts some of their flagship interdisciplinary initiatives as being "instrumental in promoting the academic career of junior scholars" but what she actually described was very distributed support to encourage interdisciplinary initiatives among doctoral and post-doctoral candidates, driven in part by the requirements of a particular funder. Furthermore, this funding initiative did not provide any form of training to support students working in an interdisciplinary way, which we have shown to be in demand with early career researchers who are seeking to develop improved "academic life skills" (Lyall and Meagher 2012).

Echoing previous findings (Meagher and Lyall 2005, 2009), one specific aspect of ECR support that was highlighted by awardholders (e.g. Norman, Gina, Reuben) was the value of dedicated post-doctoral funding for interdisciplinary researchers in order to allow them time to establish themselves as authentic interdisciplinary scholars:

> [I]t's really important for interdisciplinary researchers to be able to have a couple of years to reflect on what they've learned [to] really digest it and to make new links and to continue being interdisciplinary and to build the confidence to remain interdisciplinary because once you get into the institutions as a lecturer you're immediately identified in your title and in the courses that you teach. (Gina)

As part of their commitment to interdisciplinarity, institutions must also recognise that early career interdisciplinarians, and indeed those who are well established, require greater support for wider networking than the average researcher as their cross-discipline interests may take them to a wider range of conferences than simply the annual professional conference of their disciplinary association. Budget allowances could do more to acknowledge that funds for networking are as much the tools of their trade as the laboratory glassware of their monodisciplinary science based peers.[7]

CHANGING OUR VALUE SYSTEMS

Implementing these two new logics of interdisciplinarity—the logic of intention and the logic of commitment—would require institutions to undertake a system-wide review of human resource procedures to ensure that interdisciplinary researchers are genuinely valued and appropriately supported in their career development and progression. This is more than simply reviewing promotion procedures (although that is a necessary step); it also requires institutions to invest in research leadership and *researcher*—as well as research—development in order to grow new talent to develop teams of experienced, interdisciplinary researchers, leaders and mentors who can, in turn, nurture interdisciplinary research capacity in future generations (Lyall and Fletcher 2013).

[7] I am indebted to Professor Gabriele Bammer for this analogy.

The briefing document for the Global Research Council's (GRC) meeting on interdisciplinarity advised that

> [i]nterdisciplinary researchers in their early career stage should be encouraged to conduct [interdisciplinary research] and not be disadvantaged by departmental or publication structures. (Gleed and Marchant 2016, p. 19)

This was repeated in the GRC's final position statement:

> The development of research career paths and a global research culture where interdisciplinary contributions receive appropriate recognition in line with that accorded within traditional disciplinary boundaries is essential. GRC participants should, within the context of their research portfolios, support interdisciplinary research in institutions and for researchers at all career stages. (Global Research Council 2016)

But this is, undeniably, a "discourse of transgression" (Klein 2014) and the perceived drawbacks associated with engagement in interdisciplinarity during the early career stages stubbornly persist both in the literature (e.g. Paytan and Zoback 2007; Pfirman et al. 2007; Dooling et al. 2017; Hein et al. 2018) and in the evidence gathered from my interviews with British academics. This contradicts the supposition, offered in Chap. 1, that the situation for interdisciplinary academic careers has, in fact, improved appreciably (Callard and Fitzgerald 2015, p. 12). Tempting anyone into an interdisciplinary career without providing an adequate safety net still seems, at best, ironic if not hypocritical and possibly even unethical.

The consequences for interdisciplinarity may be far-reaching: in pointing to the "production penalty" (see Chap. 5), Leahey et al. (2017) question the wisdom of continuing to invest in such research if we do not become more attuned to the potential negative implications for individuals. If we intend to train people from the outset of their careers to be interdisciplinary—and there are excellent arguments for doing so despite the reservations of some university leaders—then it is beholden on those funding that training and research, and on those leading the academic institutions where these individuals find employment, to do it in such a way that we no longer produce scholars who have to struggle through their careers and who, at worst, may be made to feel as if they are sub-par academics as failed discipline experts. This is an argument for appreciating the softer skills that interdisciplinary training brings—developing researchers who can act as catalysts and integrators, bridge builders, and champions for social impact and engagement by being able to work with others both inside and outside of academia. Yet we still cherish the traditional academic expert who can demonstrate an extensive list of publications but cannot communicate with others beyond the narrow confines of their own specialism. Universities (from the Latin *universitas* meaning "the whole") should be broad enough to encompass both disciplines and interdisciplinarity without anyone feeling threatened; this is not an "either/or" situation. Academic life is changing for everyone, with far greater job insecurity and fragmentation of careers than in the previous generation, so it is unhelpful to dwell on the "traditional" academic profile (Åkerlind and McAlpine 2010, pp. 156–157). The academic life skills discussed in this chapter could benefit all staff, not just those following an interdisciplinary path.

Van der Zwaan (2017, p. 76) calls for greater rewards for entrepreneurship and creativity, one form of which is surely interdisciplinarity, and recommends (ibid., p. 186) that university planning should be based on "portfolios" rather than disciplines. This, he argues, requires "balancing [that word again] traditional discipline-based scholarship with interdisciplinary application to societal needs" with consequential restructuring of technical and administrative support structures (ibid., p. 241) but Vice Rectors whom I interviewed denied there was this balance or any process of negotiation (see Chap. 5). Nonetheless, much of academic life *is* a question of balance:

> [W]e're busy with a million other things, so having the time to commit to breaking down those barriers, it's going to be tricky I suppose. But there is … always time. I think it's also about motivation … because we do have time, it's just where we allocate that time. (Paterson)

If we can support, motivate and reward people appropriately in their careers then they will commit to interdisciplinarity. This does not always require loud fanfares over the launch of a new interdisciplinary strategy or institute; it requires much quieter voices working to improve the fabric of the institution and its underpinning processes and procedures. But it does also require us to reconsider what we value in academia:

> There is no intrinsic worth in being a scientist, a literary theorist, a good teacher, a good disciplinary citizen, or an interdisciplinary scholar. As a community we create our value systems. We can also alter them. (Lattuca 2001, p. 264)

Talking Points
Universities still give greater credence to the disciplinary specialist and do not yet fully appreciate the broader skill sets that individual interdisciplinarians have to offer. This necessitates a reconceptualisation of the traditional view of "academic excellence" and changes to our value systems to secure greater consistency and coherence within the governance of interdisciplinarity.

What role models do we provide for successful interdisciplinary research? Are there accidental or tacit assumptions embedded within institutions' assessment processes (including peer review and promotion decisions) that could work against interdisciplinary researchers? What steps can we all take to ensure that less-established individuals who participate in interdisciplinary research and teaching attain the necessary career milestones that will "count" towards academic promotion? What would it take to create an institutional culture that embraces and rewards disciplinary and interdisciplinary achievements equally?

References

Åkerlind, Gerlese, and Lynn McAlpine. 2010. Rethinking Preparation for Academic Careers. In *Becoming an Academic*, ed. Lynn McAlpine and Gerlese Åkerlind. Basingstoke: Palgrave Macmillan.

Barry, Andrew, Georgina Born, and Gisa Weszkalnys. 2008. Logics of Interdisciplinarity. *Economy and Society* 37 (1): 20–49.

Benson, M.H., C.D. Lippitt, R. Morrison, B. Cosens, J. Boll, B.C. Chaffin, A.K. Fremier, R. Heinse, D. Kauneckis, T.E. Link, C.E. Scruggs, M. Stone, and V. Valentin. 2016. Five Ways to Support Interdisciplinary Work Before Tenure. *Journal of Environmental Studies and Sciences* 6 (2): 260–267.

Bergland, Brita. 2017. The Incompatibility of Neoliberal University Structures and Interdisciplinary Knowledge: A Feminist Slow Scholarship Critique. *Educational Philosophy and Theory* 50 (11): 1031–1036.

Berlin, Isaiah. 1953. *The Hedgehog and the Fox: An Essay on Tolstoy's View of History*. London: Weidenfeld & Nicolson.

Blackmore, Paul, and Camille B. Kandiko. 2011. Interdisciplinarity Within an Academic Career. *Research in Post-Compulsory Education* 16 (1): 123–134.

Callard, F., and D. Fitzgerald. 2015. *Rethinking Interdisciplinarity Across the Social Sciences and Neurosciences*. Basingstoke, UK: Palgrave.

Callard, F., D. Fitzgerald, and A. Woods. 2015. Interdisciplinary Collaboration in Action: Tracking the Signal, Tracing the Noise. *Palgrave Communications* 1, article 15019.

Dooling, S., J.K. Graybill, and V. Shandas. 2017. Doctoral Student and Early Career Academic Perspectives on Interdisciplinarity. In *The Oxford Handbook of Interdisciplinarity*, ed. Robert Frodeman, Julie Thompson Klein, and C.S. Robert Pacheco, 586–600. Oxford: Oxford University Press.

Fischer, E.V., K.R.M. MacKey, D.F. Cusack, L.R.G. Desantis, L. Hartzell-Nichols, J.A. Lutz, J. Melbourne-Thomas, R. Meyer, D.A. Riveros-Iregui, C.J.B. Sorte, J.R. Taylor, and S.A. White. 2012. Is Pretenure Interdisciplinary Research a Career Risk? *Eos* 93 (32): 311–312.

Fitzgerald, D., M.M. Littlefield, K.J. Knudsen, J. Tonks, and M.J. Dietz. 2014. Ambivalence, Equivocation and the Politics of Experimental Knowledge: A Transdisciplinary Neuroscience Encounter. *Social Studies of Science* 44 (5): 701–721.

Foray, D., and A. Sors. 2014. Universities Can Lead the Way in This Era of Grand Challenges. *Research Europe*, July 5.

Frodeman, Robert. 2014. *Sustainable Knowledge*. Basingstoke: Palgrave.

Gleed, A., and D. Marchant. 2016. Interdisciplinarity. Survey Report for the Global Research Council 2016 Annual Meeting, Stockport.

Global Research Council. 2016. Statement of Principles on Interdisciplinarity. https://www.globalresearchcouncil.org/fileadmin/documents/GRC_Publications/Statement_of_Principles_on_Interdisciplinarity.pdf. Accessed 24 January 2019.

Graybill, J.K., S. Dooling, V. Shandas, J. Withey, A. Greve, and G.L. Simon. 2006. A Rough Guide to Interdisciplinarity: Graduate Student Perspectives. *BioScience* 56 (9): 757–763.

Gulbenkian Commission. 1996. *Open the Social Sciences*. Stanford, CA: Stanford University Press.

Hein, Christopher J., John E. Ten Hoeve, Sathya Gopalakrishnan, Ben Livneh, Henry D. Adams, Elizabeth K. Marino, and C. Susan Weiler. 2018. Overcoming Early Career Barriers to Interdisciplinary Climate Change Research. *Wiley Interdisciplinary Reviews: Climate Change* 9 (5): e530.

van der Hel, S. 2016. New Science for Global Sustainability? The Institutionalisation of Knowledge Co-production in Future Earth. *Environmental Science & Policy* 61: 165–175.

Holley, Karri A. 2009. Interdisciplinary Strategies As Transformative Change in Higher Education. *Innovative Higher Education* 34 (5): 331–344.

Klein, Julie Thompson. 2010. *Creating Interdisciplinary Campus Cultures*. San Francisco: Jossey Bass.

———. 2014. Discourses of Transdisciplinarity: Looking Back to the Future. *Futures* 63 (1): 68–74.

Klein, Julie Thompson, and Holly J. Falk-Krzesinski. 2017. Interdisciplinary and Collaborative Work: Framing Promotion and Tenure Practices and Policies. *Research Policy* 46 (6): 1055–1061.

Klein, Julie Thompson, Karen Moranski, and Roslyn Abt Schindler. 2016. *Guidelines for Tenure and Promotion for Interdisciplinary Faculty*. Association for Interdisciplinary Studies (AIS).

Lattuca, Lisa R. 2001. *Creating Interdisciplinarity*. Nashville: Vanderbilt University Press.

League of European Research Universities. 2016. *Interdisciplinarity and the 21st Century Research-Intensive University*. Leuven: LERU.

Leahey, E., C.M. Beckman, and T.L. Stanko. 2017. Prominent but Less Productive: The Impact of Interdisciplinarity on Scientists' Research. *Administrative Science Quarterly* 62 (1): 105–139.

Lerchenmueller, Marc J., and Olav Sorenson. 2018. The Gender Gap in Early Career Transitions in the Life Sciences. *Research Policy* 47 (6): 1007–1017.

Lindvig, Katrine. 2017. Creating Interdisciplinarity Within Monodisciplinary Structures. PhD Thesis, University of Copenhagen.

Lindvig, Katrine, and Line Hillersdal. 2018. Strategically Unclear? Organising Interdisciplinarity in an Excellence Programme of Interdisciplinary Research in Denmark. Minerva. https://doi.org/10.1007/s11024-018-9361-5.

Lyall, Catherine, and I. Fletcher. 2013. Experiments in Interdisciplinary Capacity-Building: The Successes and Challenges of Large-Scale Interdisciplinary Investments. *Science and Public Policy* 40: 1–7.

Lyall, C., and L. Meagher. 2012. A Masterclass in Interdisciplinarity: Research into Practice in Training the Next Generation of Interdisciplinary Researchers. *Futures* 44 (6): 608–617.

Martin, Paula J.S., and Stephanie Pfirman. 2017. Facilitating Interdisciplinary Scholars. In *The Oxford Handbook of Interdisciplinarity*, ed. Robert Frodeman, Julie Thompson Klein, and C.S. Robert Pacheco, 586–600. Oxford: Oxford University Press.

Meagher, Laura, and Catherine Lyall. 2005. *Evaluation of the ESRC/NERC Interdisciplinary Research Studentship Scheme*. Report to ESRC.

———. 2009. *Evaluation of ESRC/MRC Interdisciplinary Research Studentship and Post-Doctoral Fellowship Scheme*. Report to ESRC.

Meagher, L., and C. Lyall. 2013. The Invisible Made Visible: Using Impact Evaluations to Illuminate and Inform the Role of Knowledge Intermediaries. *Evidence & Policy* 9 (3): 409–418.

Mills, David. 2010. Employment Patterns in and Beyond One's Discipline. In *Becoming an Academic*, ed. Lynn McAlpine and Gerlese Åkerlind. Basingstoke: Palgrave Macmillan.

National Academy of Sciences. 2005. *Facilitating Interdisciplinary Research*. Washington, DC: National Academies Press.

Paytan, Adina, and Mary Lou Zoback. 2007. Crossing Boundaries, Hitting Barriers. *Nature* 445: 950.

Pfirman, Stephanie, and et al. 2007. *Interdisciplinary Hiring, Tenure and Promotion: Guidance for Individuals and Institutions*. Report for Council of Environmental Dean and Directors.

Razzaq, J., T. Townsend, and J. Pisapia. 2013. Towards an Understanding of Interdisciplinarity: The Case of a British University. *Issues in Interdisciplinary Studies* 31: 149–173.

Rhoten, D., and S. Pfirman. 2007. Women in Interdisciplinary Science: Exploring Preferences and Consequences. *Research Policy* 36 (1): 56–75.

Sá, Creso M. 2008. 'Interdisciplinary Strategies' in U.S. Research Universities. *Higher Education* 55: 537–552.

Skills Development Scotland. 2018. *Skills 4.0. A Skills Model to Drive Scotland's Future*. Glasgow: Skills Development Scotland.

Sobey, A.J., N.C. Townsend, C.D. Metcalf, K.D. Bruce, and F.M. Fazi. 2013. Incorporation of Early Career Researchers Within Multidisciplinary Research at Academic Institutions. *Research Evaluation* 22 (3): 169–178.

Tarrant, S.P., and L.P. Thiele. 2017. Enhancing and Promoting Interdisciplinarity in Higher Education. *Journal of Environmental Studies and Sciences* 7 (2): 355–360.

Weingart, Peter. 2000. Interdisciplinarity: The Paradoxical Discourse. In *Practising Interdisciplinarity*, ed. Peter Weingart and Nico Stehr, 25–41. Toronto: University of Toronto Press.

———. 2014. Interdisciplinarity and the New Governance of Universities. In *University Experiments in Interdisciplinarity: Obstacles and Opportunities*, ed. P. Weingart and B. Padberg. Bielefeld: Transcript Verlag.

Winskel, Mark. 2018. The Pursuit of Interdisciplinary Whole Systems Energy Research: Insights from the UK Energy Research Centre. *Energy Research & Social Science* 37: 74–84.

van der Zwaan, Bert. 2017. *Higher Education in 2040. A Global Approach*. Amsterdam: Amsterdam University Press.

CHAPTER 7

Conclusion: "The Funding Can Only Do So Much"

Hearing the Soft Voices

Our respondents were optimistic about institutional change when we evaluated the original ESRC-NERC interdisciplinary studentship scheme (Meagher and Lyall 2005) but nearly 15 years later, universities still give greater credence to the disciplinary specialist and do not yet fully appreciate the broader skill sets that individual interdisciplinarians, trained through these and similar studentships, have to offer. In a disappointing illustration of *plus ça change*,[1] my awardholder interviewees for this current study were still presenting the same issues as impediments to an interdisciplinary academic career: issues around evaluation, quality assessment, publication hurdles, unaccommodating institutional structures and procedures, and a lack of career development support and guidance.

As well as this slow pace of change, my conversations with awardholders and institutional leaders revealed some stark misalignments within the systems of governance for interdisciplinary careers. Vice Rectors of Research (the "loud voices" in my sample) extolled strategic interdisciplinary research investments, whereas awardholder interviewees (the "soft voices") reflected on the greater durability of more bottom up approaches to interdisciplinary research while recognising that such attitudes were now largely antithetical to the mores and strictures of modern academia (see Chap. 5 on "slow research").

---

[1] *Plus ça change plus c'est la même chose*: the more it changes, the more it stays the same.

© The Author(s) 2019
C. Lyall, *Being an Interdisciplinary Academic*,
https://doi.org/10.1007/978-3-030-18659-3_7

As just one example of the mixed messages that our early career researchers receive about the value of an interdisciplinary career, Helena very clearly articulated the tension between the loud and soft voices within her university when she described the realities of developing and maintaining her discipline- and organisation-spanning career and sincerely hoped for some institutional memory so that her trailblazing would not be for nought. Yet these interviews demonstrated that we could be making much better use of the interdisciplinary community that we have created in order to share good practice and lessons learned about the progress and status of interdisciplinarity within the academy.

The ambiguities and conflicting rhetorics presented in these interviews prompted me to muse on the phrase "choose your institution wisely" but, as Gina cautioned, it is hard to be discerning when "everyone's talking the interdisciplinary talk at the moment". The data presented in this book have shown how interdisciplinary academic careers are built in practice and the very evident challenges that these colleagues continue to face. Indeed, a focus on the barriers and disincentives seems to be the hallmark of much writing on interdisciplinarity. But if we truly want to commit to this mode of working, we have to find ways of overcoming the impasse that exists between policy demands for solutions from interdisciplinary research and the institutional obstacles to interdisciplinary education and interdisciplinary academic careers. The quotation in the title of this chapter, which arose when I was discussing with SR3 how universities value interdisciplinary researchers, epitomises the responsibility that we all share as a research community—researchers, institutional leaders, funding agencies and learned and professional societies—to consider the standing of interdisciplinary research and researchers within our universities in order to address these mixed messages.

The equivocation that research leaders evince, combined with funders' apparent abnegation of responsibility for career outcomes or "unintended consequences" (SR3, Chap. 3), cry out for clearer intentions and greater commitment (see Chap. 6) so that our universities can demonstrate to their staff that they unambiguously support interdisciplinarity. In calling for more change, the quiet voices seek both greater attention to the "softer" skills (e.g. effective mentoring) and practical support (e.g. postdoctoral funding to establish truly interdisciplinary careers).

This equivocation is nowhere more evident than in the matter of "when to become interdisciplinary" (see Chap. 4). Without disciplines there can be no "interdisciplinarity" so, we are left with the tough, fundamental question of whether we seek to enhance interdisciplinary capabilities by training early career researchers who are true interdisciplinary "hybrids" or by giving an interdisciplinary orientation to discipline-grounded researchers. This was the discussion about "hybridisation versus sensitisation" in Chap. 4 where I marshalled arguments drawn from the sociology of scientific knowledge to make the case that true interdisciplinarians offer much more than simply an accumulation of discipline-based knowledge.

Long years of tradition within the university sector militate against a complete overhaul of structures, not least because higher education in the twenty-first century is undergoing a number of changes (e.g. van der Zwaan 2017) and such new configurations might not remain fit for purpose longer term. Rather than radically reconceptualising our universities (Crow and Dabars 2015, passim.), it is more realistic to suggest a re-tuning or a recalibration, not a wholesale redesign process. Nonetheless, in the context of increasing interdisciplinarity, now is the time to start a debate about how we might design more flexible and responsive university governance systems to nurture "institutionalized serendipity" as advanced by Merton (2004, see Chap. 5) and to consider how we might reframe universities in future "as if interdisciplinarity mattered" (Bina 2017).

Academic departments are seen as a "source of inertia" within universities (Biancani et al. 2018) and "bulwarks against change" (Boardman and Bozeman 2007) and awardholders and research leaders alike underlined the problems of very scattered or siloed campuses. As discussed in Chap. 5, countering this dispersal problem requires resources—in the form of time, space *and* money—to facilitate greater informal networking, recognising that such engagements are examples of slow research that, most likely, will not lead to immediate, tangible returns. One concrete proposal to build greater linkages across universities that I heard during interviews could take the form of internal secondments for both academic and administrative staff to engender a greater appreciation of the myriad styles of working that most universities exhibit.

In parallel, as well as reconceptualising interdisciplinary scholarship and encouraging universities to take a more encompassing view of an academic career (Chap. 6), interdisciplinary colleagues could be supported to present their skills in smarter ways so that they are confident in evidencing different forms of "excellence". These "academic life skills" include identifying and holding on to the coherent "golden thread" that awardholders spoke about (Chap. 2) so that even those who have followed the interdisciplinary path from the start, can offer a cogent (if sometimes post hoc) rationalisation of their contribution to academic excellence.

Starting our own debate in the UK about interdisciplinary "tenure" would provide colleagues with more contextualised information to compensate for the predominance of US literature in this area. Chapter 3 identified the "perpetual research fellow problem", which is intensified for interdisciplinarians by the lack of teaching opportunities. This may not change until interdisciplinary teaching programmes become more established at undergraduate level in the UK (see Lyall et al. 2015; Gombrich and Hogan 2017) but, in the interim, ought we to question whether a teaching role should be the only route to a secure university post if interdisciplinary research expertise does really merit the prominence that research funders and research leaders claim?

Inappropriate leadership at project or programme level can result in an imperfect form of interdisciplinarity where, for example, high-quality social science is squeezed out and researchers[2] experience the deskilling aspects of providing a social science "subordination-service" role (Barry et al. 2008) in a supposedly interdisciplinary environment. Given awardholders' observations about how a research culture can change with leadership, it is disingenuous of Vice Rectors to claim that "our academics are completely free to pursue whatever research they wish" (VR2) when the university leadership is responsible for creating an environment that then permeates the institution, which either enables or confounds interdisciplinarity. This is not necessarily a question about overt forms of leadership but the atmosphere that research leaders create. Too often, we have "the wrong people" in leadership positions, assuming that "the elite of the establishment" have the skills to lead interdisciplinary initiatives (Gina). Perhaps we will only see real institutional change once my awardholder interviewees and their ilk become university leaders:

> I think it's important to then have people that understand interdisciplinarity, truly understand it, at high levels of, whether it's academic leadership or management, which I suppose is still quite unusual because interdisciplinarity I feel is much more common within early career people, and certainly within PhD cohorts even more so now. So they can understand, not so much just having people with a specific discipline working together in

[2] Notably but not exclusively evidenced by those working in the medical sciences in my sample.

interdisciplinary teams but understanding what it is to have individuals that are truly interdisciplinary, so I think it's important to have role models. (Fiona)

How likely this progression is, given the obstacles and apparently unplanned nature of some of these careers (see Chap. 2), is another matter.

Nevertheless, awardholders attest to the fact that research leaders and research funders could be doing more to learn from the experiences of interdisciplinary research practitioners. This requires a whole system approach (see Chap. 6 on the logic of intention and the logic of commitment). Yet, currently, research leaders and research funders are essentially only intervening at a rhetorical or "symbolic" level in the form of new interdisciplinary institutions and initiatives. While such initiatives may release resources to fund interdisciplinary research, awardholder interviewees saw this as the least successful means of effecting institutional change if it was not accompanied by refinements to university procedures that impact on the individual academic in terms of administration, promotion and so on.

A Systemic Approach

Truly systemic change (see also Rhoten 2004) relates to how we value and evaluate interdisciplinarity. This requires resourcing but also deep cultural change within the university sector. Embedding such a systemic approach to interdisciplinary research will also entail greater involvement from funders. This leadership role tends to be underplayed, in the UK at least, perhaps because funders have a tendency to take shelter behind the "Haldane Principle".[3] Up to this point, the attention of research funders has primarily focused on peer review and evaluation processes with some funding agencies beginning to examine issues of fairness and parity in review processes for interdisciplinary research. Such considerations include the composition of review panels, the selection of external reviewers, the design of the review process[4] and, in some cases, discussions about greater partnership and dialogue between applicants and reviewers (Lyall and King 2013). While there are evident improvements being trialled by some

---

[3] See www.ukri.org/research/themes-and-programmes/haldane/ (accessed 17/1/19).
[4] For example, allowing for longer proposals, more flexible timetables and dedicated budgets for network building and travel to a wider range of conferences.

funders,[5] an improved understanding of the nature of interdisciplinary careers—the individual interdisciplinarians versus the collaborative discipline expert—and the different implications this has for both the research and the researcher, is still called for. This understanding would be reinforced if accompanied by a greater knowledge of the "cognitive processes of knowledge integration" (Huutoniemi et al. 2010) at both the individual and team level.

All of this presents funders with the task of balancing flexibility and parity with others forms of (monodisciplinary) research and also with cost effectiveness of review processes. As trends for interdisciplinary research increase, this will also have an impact on teaching and training in order to inculcate the "soft skills" or "meta-skills" (Skills Development Scotland 2018) in the form of leadership, creativity, communication and so on that facilitate interdisciplinary collaboration (van der Zwaan 2017, p. 229). Above all, funders need to be more mindful of the impact of interdisciplinarity on academic careers than hitherto. In the case of individual interdisciplinarians, this includes greater awareness of support for career trajectories by appropriate funding throughout the academic life course, bearing in mind Leahey et al.'s, (2017) admonition of the impropriety of continuing to fund interdisciplinary research if we fail to take proper cognisance of its negative implications for academic careers (see Chap. 6).

"BOTH SHOULD BE POSSIBLE"

Interdisciplinarity is not for everyone and nor should it be in a thriving, multidimensional university. But, just as we have moved from a position that called for a unity of knowledge (Wilson 1999) to one that recognises interdisciplinarity as a heterogeneous "field of differences" (Klein 2014; Barry and Born 2013), so too are there calls for universities to adopt a diversity of forms that can adapt to change (van der Zwaan 2017, p. 243). So, if we do want to build a stronger interdisciplinary future and one that will have impact beyond our universities, what can academic institutions do to facilitate this?

---

[5] From informal discussions with a number of representatives of funding agencies, these include such aspects as learning events for panellists, improved training for reviewers and for those who design programmes, and pooled peer reviewer databases to facilitate access to a wider range of interdisciplinary experts.

First, we must stop seeing interdisciplinarity as an epiphenomenon[6]: the prevailing ethos within research-intensive universities is discipline excellence first, then interdisciplinary collaboration. If we are to nurture and indeed benefit from the expertise of true interdisciplinarians, interdisciplinarity has to be entrenched and embedded rather than epiphenomenal.

Secondly, we might better acknowledge the "mission for insurgency" that is inherent in interdisciplinarity (Klein 2010, p. 123). If we want to harness the creative potential of interdisciplinary research, how could we better manage the contradictions between the institutionalisation of interdisciplinarity and supporting that mission for insurgency so that we do not impede it with bureaucracy? Too often we intervene at the wrong levels: less grand strategy and more attention to the basics are required. Inappropriate peer review is an overarching, system-wide problem and, at local levels, administration, recruitment and promotion procedures require attention. If we can address these issues, people will feel more secure following an interdisciplinary career. In order to do so, we could strive to:

- share experiences, intelligence and resources to foster organisational learning
- address the administrative barriers, disincentives and mixed messages within our own institutions and more broadly
- volunteer our time to contribute to peer review so that interdisciplinary evaluation processes are fit for purpose
- provide better training, mentoring and institutional support for interdisciplinary research leaders at all levels (whether they lead small projects or large research institutes), interdisciplinary teachers and, especially, interdisciplinary early career researchers so that there is parity of opportunity, progression and reward

With these steps we could begin to turn interdisciplinary research from something that still risks being largely symbolic into something that is systemic within our institutions. And in so doing, harness the benefits of lasting, world-class interdisciplinary research for both societal and academic progress.

In summary, such a move requires (1) research policymakers and funding agencies, who promote interdisciplinarity, to develop a greater

---

[6] An epiphenomenon is a secondary phenomenon accompanying another and caused by it. It is primarily used to describe medical conditions.

awareness of, and appropriate responses to, the potentially negative conse-quences for academic careers and (2) the universities that employ such staff to be more consistent in aligning their avowed support for interdisci-plinarity with their procedures and attitudes towards "excellence". In call-ing for this greater coherence within the university system, I return to the notion of "balance", which has been an underlying motif throughout the book, and leave the final word to one of the Vice Rectors of Research:

> For the good of the university and for the good of research and for the good of our education … we should not stick to one possible path and to one possible model of education and research. I'm not saying to throw away all of it. Not at all. But both should be possible. (VR7)

REFERENCES

Barry, Andrew, and Georgina Born. 2013. Interdisciplinarity. Reconfigurations of the Social and Natural Sciences. In *Interdisciplinarity. Reconfigurations of the Social and Natural Sciences*, ed. Andrew Barry and Georgina Born, 1–56. Abingdon: Routledge.

Barry, Andrew, Georgina Born, and Gisa Weszkalnys. 2008. Logics of Interdisciplinarity. *Economy and Society* 37 (1): 20–49.

Biancani, Susan, Linus Dahlander, Daniel A. McFarland, and Sanne Smith. 2018. Superstars in the Making? The Broad Effects of Interdisciplinary Centers. *Research Policy* 47 (3): 543–557.

Bina, O. (2017) Thinking About the Future of Universities: Highlights from Our Discussions at the TD Net Conference, 17 November, INTREPID COST Action TD 1408. http://www.intrepid-cost.eu. Accessed 27 January 2019.

Boardman, Craig, and Barry Bozeman. 2007. Role Strain in University Research Centers. *The Journal of Higher Education* 78 (4): 430–463.

Crow, M., and W. Dabars. 2015. *Designing the New American University*. Baltimore: Johns Hopkins University Press.

Gombrich, C., and M. Hogan. 2017. Interdisciplinarity and the Student Voice. In *The Oxford Handbook of Interdisciplinarity*, ed. R. Frodeman, J.T. Klein, and R.C.S. Pacheco, 544–557. Oxford: Oxford University Press.

Huutoniemi, Katri, Julie Thompson Klein, Henrik Bruun, and Janne Hukkinen. 2010. Analyzing Interdisciplinarity: Typology and Indicators. *Research Policy* 39 (1): 79–88.

Klein, Julie Thompson. 2010. *Creating Interdisciplinary Campus Cultures*. San Francisco: Jossey Bass.

———. 2014. Discourses of Transdisciplinarity: Looking Back to the Future. *Futures* 63 (1): 68–74.

Leahey, E., C.M. Beckman, and T.L. Stanko. 2017. Prominent but Less Productive: The Impact of Interdisciplinarity on Scientists' Research. *Administrative Science Quarterly* 62 (1): 105–139.

Lyall, Catherine, and Emma King. 2013. International Good Practice in the Peer Review of Interdisciplinary Research. Report to the RCUK Research Directors Group.

Lyall, C., L. Meagher, J. Bandola, and A. Kettle. 2015. Interdisciplinary Provision in Higher Education: Current and Future Challenges. Report to Higher Education Academy.

Meagher, Laura, and Catherine Lyall. 2005. Evaluation of the ESRC/NERC Interdisciplinary Research Studentship Scheme. Report to ESRC.

Merton, R.K. 2004. Afterword. In *Autobiographical Reflections on the Travels and Adventures of Serendipity in the Travels and Adventures of Serendipity: A Study in Sociological Semantics and the Sociology of Science*, ed. R.K. Merton and E. Barber. Princeton: Princeton University Press.

Rhoten, Diana. 2004. Interdisciplinary Research: Trend or Transition. *Items and Issues* 5 (1–2): 6–11.

Skills Development Scotland. 2018. *Skills 4.0. A Skills Model to Drive Scotland's Future*. Glasgow: Skills Development Scotland.

Wilson, Edward O. 1999. *Consilience. The Unity of Knowledge*. London: Abacus.

van der Zwaan, Bert. 2017. *Higher Education in 2040. A Global Approach*. Amsterdam: Amsterdam University Press.

APPENDIX A: FURTHER READING

The following reading list introduces selected key topics within interdisciplinary (and transdisciplinary) research for a wide audience including researchers from varied disciplines, research funders, research policymakers and university leaders.

SHORT READS

Series of four-page guides available from http://tinyurl.com/idwiki

1. A Short Guide to Developing Interdisciplinary Research Proposals
2. A Short Guide to Reviewing Interdisciplinary Research Proposals
3. A Short Guide to Building and Managing Interdisciplinary Research Teams
4. A Short Guide to Supervising Interdisciplinary PhDs
5. A Short Guide to Troubleshooting Some Common Interdisciplinary Research Management Challenges
6. A Short Guide to Designing Interdisciplinary Research for Policy and Practice
7. A Short Guide to Developing Interdisciplinary Strategies for Research Groups
8. A Short Guide for Funders of Interdisciplinary Research
9. A Short Guide to Evaluating Interdisciplinary Research
10. A Short Guide to Leading Interdisciplinary Initiatives
11. A Short Guide to Exploring Interdisciplinary Careers

© The Author(s) 2019
C. Lyall, *Being an Interdisciplinary Academic*,
https://doi.org/10.1007/978-3-030-18659-3

Handbooks, Anthologies and Overviews

Frodeman, R., et al., eds. 2017. *The Oxford Handbook of Interdisciplinarity.* Oxford: Oxford University Press.

Hirsch Hadorn, G., et al., eds. 2008. *Handbook of Transdisciplinary Research.* Heidelberg: Springer.

Lyall, C., et al. 2011. *Interdisciplinary Research Journeys. Practical Strategies for Capturing Creativity.* London: Bloomsbury Academic.

Vienni, B., et al., eds. 2015. *Encuentros sobre Interdisciplina.* Montevideo, Espacio Interdisciplinario de la Universidad de la Republica (in Spanish).

Histories and Typologies of Interdisciplinarity

Barry, A., et al. 2008. Logics of Interdisciplinarity. *Economy and Society* 37 (1): 20–49.

Huutoniemi, K., et al. 2010. Analyzing Interdisciplinarity: Typology and Indicators. *Research Policy* 39 (1): 79–88.

Klein, J.T. 1990. *Interdisciplinarity – History, Theory and Practice.* Detroit: Wayne State University Press.

Lowe, P., et al. 2013. Why Social Scientists Should Engage with Natural Scientists. *Contemporary Social Science: Journal of the Academy of Social Sciences* 8 (3): 207–222.

Advice on Interdisciplinary Careers

Martin, P.J.S., and S. Pfirman. 2017. Facilitating Interdisciplinary Scholars. In *The Oxford Handbook of Interdisciplinarity*, ed. R. Frodeman, J.T. Klein, and R.C.S. Pacheco, 586–600. Oxford: Oxford University Press.

Pfirman, S., and M. Begg. 2012. Troubled by Interdisciplinarity? *Science*, April 6.

Evaluation and Peer Review

Lyall, C., and E. King. 2013. International Good Practice in the Peer Review of Interdisciplinary Research, Report to the RCUK Research Directors Group.

Pohl, C., et al. 2011. Questions to Evaluate Inter- and Transdisciplinary Research Proposals. Bern, Working Paper, td-net for Transdisciplinary Research.

WEB-BASED TOOL KITS AND RESOURCE REPOSITORIES

About Interdisciplinarity https://sites.google.com/a/ualberta.ca/rick-szostak/research/about-interdisciplinarity
AIS Association for Interdisciplinary Studies https://oakland.edu/ais/
i2S Integration and Implementation Sciences https://i2s.anu.edu.au

See also I2S Insights (blog) https://i2insights.org including occasional synthesis blog posts https://i2insights.org/tag/synthesis-blog-post/

td-net Network for Transdisciplinary Research www.transdisciplinarity.ch

See also td-net toolbox https://naturalsciences.ch/topics/co-producing_knowledge/td-net_toolbox and Tour d'Horizon of Literature http://www.transdisciplinarity.ch/en/td-net/Publikationen/Tour-d-Horizon.html

Team Science Toolkit www.teamsciencetoolkit.cancer.gov

Appendix B: Research Design

The research design for this study adopted a qualitative approach because, for this topic, I wanted to hear the voices of those affected by the issue of interdisciplinary academic careers. As noted in Chap. 1, the research design sought out both the "loud" voices of university leaders and the "soft" voices of interdisciplinary researchers.

Selection of Informants

The first phase of these interviews (conducted February–April 2018) involved 22 academics based in British universities whose doctoral studies had been funded by one of two joint Research Council studentship schemes.[1] The sample for these "awardholder interviewees" was identified by desk research, searching biographical details on public domain university websites and acknowledgements in online PhD theses and other scholarly publications for mentions of this studentship award.

To ensure a good breadth of experience, I then used a range of sampling criteria, including

---

[1] Funded by the Economic and Social Research Council (ESRC) and the Natural Environment Research Council (NERC) and by the Economic and Social Research Council and the Medical Research Council (MRC) respectively.

© The Author(s) 2019
C. Lyall, *Being an Interdisciplinary Academic*,
https://doi.org/10.1007/978-3-030-18659-3

- Date of PhD award
- Current position (Professor, Senior Lecturer or Reader, Lecturer, Researcher)
- Type of university
- Gender
- ESRC/NERC or ESRC/MRC funding

The demographic profile of these interviewees is summarised in Table B.1. I was initially concerned about the predominance of women in my sample but was reminded that 80% of ESRC/MRC studentship awards had gone to women (Meagher and Lyall 2009, p. 20).

The university sector in the UK is quite heterogeneous. Collini (2012, Chapter 2) reminds us that, at the time of the French Revolution, there were only seven universities in the UK, but that we have since seen waves of growth with the birth of "the civic universities" of the Victorian era, "the plate glass universities" in the 1960s, and "the post 1992s" when many polytechnics gained university status. I chose to focus on the leading research intensive universities (known as the Russell Group[2]) in order to reduce some of the variation between different types of UK universities and in order to give greater comparability with my second interview sample, described below. Furthermore, we had previously analysed Russell Group university strategic plans (Bandola and Lyall 2015) and knew that the vast majority[3] mentioned interdisciplinarity in some form in their published strategies.

Having identified a sample of awardholders, the uptake of invitations to participate in a research interview was enthusiastic suggesting that interdisciplinary careers are a "live" topic among British academic colleagues.

In the second phase of interviews, termed the "leadership interviews" and conducted May–June 2018, I visited a sample of universities who are members of the League of European Research Universities (LERU).[4] The focus of these interviews was to probe how research-intensive universities' vision for interdisciplinarity might impact on career development.

---

[2] https://russellgroup.ac.uk (accessed on 7/1/19).
[3] That is, 23 out of the 24 member universities and quite possibly all as the 24th strategic plan was not available at the time of our 2015 study.
[4] www.leru.org (accessed on 7/1/19).

Table B.1 Demographic profile of awardholder interviewees

Name[a]	Gender	PhD funder	Moved from PhD host?	Year of PhD award	Russell Group?	Job category[b]	Career stage[c]
Anna	F	ESRC-MRC	Y	2010	N	Senior Lecturer	Senior
Belinda	F	ESRC-MRC	Y	2010	Y	Researcher	Mid
Carina	F	ESRC-MRC	N	2008	Y	Lecturer	Mid
Diana	F	ESRC-MRC	Y	2009	Y	Reader	Senior
Erica	F	ESRC-MRC	N	2014	Y	Researcher	Early
Fiona	F	ESRC-NERC	Y	2009	Y	Senior Lecturer	Senior
Gina	F	ESRC-NERC	Y	2006	N	Senior Lecturer	Senior
Helena	F	ESRC-MRC	Y	2009	Y	Lecturer	Mid
Iona	F	ESRC-MRC	Y	2008	Y	Researcher	Mid
Julia	F	ESRC-MRC	N	2011	Y	Researcher	Mid
Katya	F	ESRC-MRC	N	2014	Y	Researcher	Early
Louisa	F	ESRC-NERC	Y	2005	N	Senior Lecturer	Senior
Mariana	F	ESRC-NERC	Y	2008	Y	Researcher	Mid
Norman	M	ESRC-NERC	Y	2006	Y	Lecturer	Mid
Owen	M	ESRC-NERC	N	2007	Y	Senior Lecturer	Senior
Paterson	M	ESRC-MRC	Y	2009	N	Senior Lecturer	Senior
Quentin	M	ESRC-NERC	Y	2003	Y	Professor	Senior
Reuben	M	ESRC-NERC	Y	2009	Y	Senior Lecturer	Senior
Selina	F	ESRC-MRC	N	2011	N	Researcher	Mid
Tristan	M	ESRC-NERC	Y	2004	N	Reader	Senior
Una	F	ESRC-NERC	N	2008	N	Researcher	Mid
Vera	F	ESRC-NERC	N	2003	N	Senior Lecturer	Senior

[a]All of these names are pseudonyms and unrelated to the interviewees' actual names

[b]The term "researcher" here encompasses a range of actual job titles and reflects the fact that the postholder is employed on a fixed-term contract (as revealed in the pre-interview survey) whereas all other postholders are on open contracts

[c]My assessment of career stage is based primarily on the number of years since the award of the PhD although in the UK there is no fixed agreement on when one stops being an "Early Career Researcher" as different funders apply different criteria

In the case of the leadership interviews, prior discussion with the LERU office had helped to identify Vice Rectors of Research[5] and other senior university figures who had been particularly engaged in discussions leading to the publication of their report on interdisciplinary research (LERU 2016) and were therefore deemed to be somewhat sensitised to the topic of interdisciplinary careers in academia. These nine individuals, plus another senior figure from one of the relevant UK research funding agencies, formed the second part of the interview sample.

INTERVIEWS

Interviews were conducted in person (by preference) or by Skype or telephone where required by logistics and availability. Interviews were "semi-structured" in the sense that they were steered by a topic guide but did not all follow the same ordering of questions. The topic guide for the awardholders took interviewees through key stages of their careers and asked them about their experiences with their current university. The topic guide for the leadership interviews was based on a close reading of the LERU report (ibid.) and informed by initial analysis of some of the themes emerging from awardholder interviews.

The majority of these interviews lasted around 60 minutes and all of my interviewees agreed to be audio recorded. These recordings were then transcribed verbatim by professional transcribers.

Prior to interviews, informants were emailed an information sheet about the project and an informed consent procedure. In the case of awardholder interviewees, they were also asked to send me a copy of their current CV and to complete a very short online survey to provide information about key career landmarks (e.g. time to complete PhD, number and duration of post-doctoral positions and, where appropriate, date of first publication, date of appointment to first lectureship, date of first grant as Principal Investigator, date appointed to a personal chair). This information provided some background and context that facilitated the subsequent interviews.

---

[5] These university senior management positions are variously termed Pro-Vice Chancellor, Provost or Vice Principal in the UK, Vice-President in the US and Pro-Rector in some other European universities, so I have settled on the term "Vice Rector", which is the terminology used by LERU.

In order to encourage frank and open discussion, I assured all of my awardholder interviewees of anonymity and each is therefore identified only by a pseudonym. Prior to analysis, all possible identifiers, such as their current or previous universities, were deleted from the transcripts. In some cases this anonymisation process also required omission of some references to their specific research topics and so on where this might have identified the individual.

The majority of the Vice Rectors whom I interviewed were willing to speak "on the record" but, as the remaining respondents in this sample (plus one of the Vice Rectors) requested anonymity, I decided to apply this to all of these interviews. Vice Rectors are therefore identified as VR1–VR7 and the remaining three senior representatives as SR1–SR3. As women were in the minority in my leadership sample, I have chosen to identify all of my leadership respondents with female pronouns in order to preserve anonymity.

The research topic and research participants were assessed as being ethically unproblematic and the research received ethical approval from the University of Edinburgh's School of Social and Political Science Research Ethics Committee.[6] Prior to interview, each participant was asked to read and sign an informed consent form; in the case of telephone or Skype interviews, oral consent or an electronic signature were accepted.

ANALYSIS

The computer-aided qualitative data analysis software, NVivo,[7] was used as a document management and qualitative data analysis tool. The data analysis took the form of several iterations of thematic coding using a mix of pre-established codes derived from the interview topic guide and a range of "in-vivo" or "grounded" codes that emerged from the data. This process of pattern recognition and data reduction led initially to descriptive analysis followed by the emergence of explanatory analysis.

Given my long engagement with the topic and familiarity with the literature, the approach to data analysis was, in reality, as we have noted elsewhere (King and Lyall 2018), a mixed one, probably reflecting both the positivist and pragmatist epistemological underpinnings of grounded

---

[6] www.sps.ed.ac.uk/research/research_ethics (accessed on 7/1/19).
[7] www.qsrinternational.com/nvivo/home (accessed on 7/1/19).

theory (Charmaz 2014). Grounded theory also allowed for data collection to take place iteratively (Strauss and Corbin 1994), most notably with findings from early awardholder interviews contributing to questions asked during the later stages of data collection and informing the structure of the topic guide for the leadership interviews.

In reporting these qualitative data I have had to deal with the usual challenges of trying to retain complexity and nuance despite the need to condense and synthesise. In presenting a textual commentary of my findings, I have tried to celebrate the voices of the individuals whom I interviewed wherever possible in order to honour their career struggles and therefore use direct quotations to preserve the language, terms and concepts that my informants used.

REFERENCES

Bandola, J., and C. Lyall. 2015. *Interdisciplinarity in the Strategic Documents of the Russell Group Universities.* University of Edinburgh. Report to Researcher Experience Committee.

Charmaz, K. 2014. *Constructing Grounded Theory.* Los Angeles: Sage.

Collini, Stefan. 2012. *What Are Universities For?* London: Penguin.

King, E., and C. Lyall. 2018. What's in a Name: Are Cultured Red Blood Cells 'Natural'? *Sociology of Health and Illness* 40 (4): 687–701.

League of European Research Universities. 2016. *Interdisciplinarity and the 21st Century Research-Intensive University.* Leuven: LERU.

Meagher, Laura, and Catherine Lyall. 2009. Evaluation of ESRC/MRC Interdisciplinary Research Studentship and Post-Doctoral Fellowship Scheme. Report to ESRC.

Strauss, A.L., and J. Corbin. 1994. Grounded Theory Methodology. In *Handbook of Qualitative Research,* ed. N.K. Denzin and Y.S. Lincoln. London: Sage.

Index[1]

[1] Note: Page numbers followed by 'n' refer to notes.

Printed by Printforce, the Netherlands